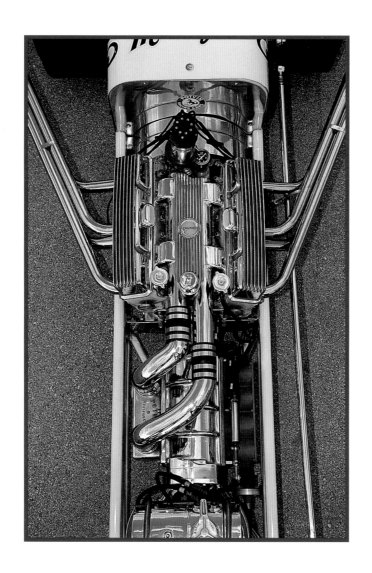

AMERICAN DRAG RACING

ROBERT GENAT

MBI Publishing Company

Dedication

To Wally Parks—the man with the vision.

First published in 2001 by MBI Publishing Company
Galtier Plaza, Suite 200, 380 Jackson Street,
St. Paul, MN 55101-3885 USA

MBI Publishing Company books are also available at discounts in bulk quantity for industrial or sales-promotional use. For details write to Special Sales Manager at
Motorbooks International Wholesalers & Distributors
Galtier Plaza, Suite 200, 380 Jackson Street,
St. Paul, MN 55101-3885 USA

Library of Congress Cataloging-in-Publication Data
Genat, Robert.
    American drag racing / Robert Genat.
        p. cm.
    Includes index.
    ISBN 0-7603-0871-3 (hard : alk. paper)
    1. Drag racing—United States—History. I. Title.
GV1029.3 .G46 2001
796.72—dc21   2001018701

On the front cover: Driver Carl Olson sits in Mike Kuhl's Top Fuel dragster on Pomona's starting line. He's trying to get a good view of the track while looking around the supercharged Hemi engine. Running a 98 percent mixture of nitromethane produces thousands of horsepower and white-hot flames from the headers.

On the frontis piece: The Mooneyes dragster was a work of art. During the process of building this exquisite dragster, Dean Moon cleared his parts shelf. The finned valve covers were a Moon product, and the Potvin crankshaft blower drive was sold along with the famous Moon fuel tank.

On the title page: Dragmaster built one of the finest race car chassis ever produced. It was lightweight and handled beautifully. Both of these are examples of the last version produced, called the "Dart." It featured a longer wheelbase than previous models. In the background is the Dragmaster Dart, the factory team car and winner of the 1962 Winternationals. In the foreground is the Phil Parker car, which set the A/Dragster elapsed time record of 8.95 seconds at the 1964 U.S. Nationals.

On the back cover: Top: Ford Motor Company was heavily involved in all types of automobile racing in 1965. In addition to sweeping the Indy 500 and cleaning up in the NASCAR points standings, Ford-powered cars left an indelible mark on drag racing. Unable to run its new SOHC 427 in NASCAR, Ford redirected its efforts for that engine to drag racing. Connie Kalitta broke the 200 mile per hour barrier in his Ford SOHC powered dragster. In addition, SOHC powered Mustangs and Galaxies rewrote drag racing's record books. *Ford Motor Company*

Bottom: In 1970, Mickey Thompson was heavily involved with Ford Motor Company. He asked Nye Frank, one of the craftsmen in his shop, to build this 1970 Mustang Mach I Funny Car. This car was unusual because the chassis was a monocoque design with an aluminum lower tub similar to an Indy car. Because of the unique design, only the top portion of the body opened. This car was powered by a supercharged Ford Boss 429 engine.

Edited by Paul Johnson
Designed by Katie Sonmor
Author photo by Joe Veraldi
Printed in China

CONTENTS

ACKNOWLEDGMENTS

The creation of a book such as this was much like running an AA/Fuel Dragster in the 1960s. The driver may have had his name on the side of the car, but he couldn't do it all, and neither could I. To get a car running back then, it took a chassis builder, a body builder, an engine builder, and a tuner. At the track, it took a few others helping with menial tasks in the pits. This book, like one of those dragsters, required a full staff of builders, tuners, and helpers to get me to the starting line. Some people answered questions, someone else found a historic photo, others shared large collections of photos, and another gave me a phone number of a legend to call. Some helped me push race cars for a photo shoot, and others took the time out of their busy days to sit for a lengthy interview. Some names will be instantly recognizable and others will not, but every one of the following people contributed to this book in a memorable way and I can't thank them enough: Greg Sharp, Steve Gibbs, Tommy Ivo,

Wally Parks, Mike Kuhl, Carl Olson, Steve Davis, Don Garlits, Bill Pitts, Kent Fuller, Tom Morris, Ed McCulloch, Pete Garamonne, Jess Van Deventer, Bob Mosher, Tony Nancy, Don Prudhomme, Al Lugo, Larry Weiner, Norm Kraus, Anthony Lugo, the late Leslie Lovett, Larry Faust, Bob Muravez, Don Nicholson, Joe Veraldi, John Buttera, Don Schumacher, Joaquin Arnett, Charlie DiBari, Randy Williams, Pamela Przywara, Bruce Meyer, Steve Hendrickson, Tom Allen, Don Cox, Jim Wangers, Shirley Muldowney, Lisa Barrow, Brian Mullane, Dan LaCroix, Marvin T. Smith, Larry Davis, Gene Mooneyham, Brad Gallant, Mickey Weise, Pete Starrett, Bert Brown, John Logghe, the late Steve Evans, Scott Tieman, John Force, Walt Knoch, Jerry Dodson, Dave Crane, Tom Sturm, Vern Tratechaud, James Genat, Bob Gladstone, Bud Barnes, Jeff Peterson, Elwood Peterson, Gary Jankowski, Kirk Richardson and Joel Naprestek. A special thanks to Dave McClelland, drag racing's premier announcer, for writing the foreword for this book.

FOREWORD

Little did I realize that day in 1959 would have such a dramatic impact on my life. I climbed a set of short, rickety stairs onto a flatbed trailer parked beside an Arkansas airport runway, picked up a microphone, and started describing the racing action unfolding just below me. I had been attending drag-racing events for four years, both as a racer and a spectator, but had never gotten involved in the mechanics of race presentation. That event in 1959 started a career as a drag-race announcer, television commentator, and racetrack manager that has encompassed six different decades and literally tens of thousands of races.

The sport of drag racing was still in its infancy in the late 1950s. Spawned from the dry lake beds of California, the Bonneville Salt Flats in Utah, and the streets of America, drag racing provided the perfect outlet for the competitive spirit of America's hot rodding youth. Racing for the fastest speed possible was exciting indeed, but the wide-open spaces best suited for such competition were in short supply outside of the Far West. In other parts of the country, hot rodders wheeling their personalized machines used the only smooth surface that was readily available.

Street racing seemed to be the hobby of choice among the youthful drivers of the era. No community was immune, no geographical section untouched by the rapidly spreading phenomenon of hot rodding and racing. Until the birth of organized drag racing, the streets of America hosted competitive action, much to the dismay of the local constabulary and citizenry.

While Southern California is regarded as the birthplace of drag racing, it wasn't long before the sport, under the direction of the National Hot Rod Association, began creating the same unbridled excitement at many locations throughout the country. Those early racetracks were rudimentary at best, with little or no fan amenities and even less in the way of improvements to whatever surface existed. The super tracks were decades away.

Yet the racer could hardly believe his good fortune—a track that catered to his type of action, with no oncoming traffic, no cross streets, and no curbs lined with people. Even better, no police and few rules. While this euphoric period formed the foundation of the sport as we know it today, the need for better safety rules for drivers and the growing number of spectators became obvious. Although some racers bridled at what they considered an intrusion into their fun, the sport needed some structure to its regulations and operating procedures.

In the beginning, the vehicles in competition matched the racetracks for lack of sophistication. Most of the races involved street-driven vehicles, their owner-drivers trying to settle once and for all the age-old question of whose car was the fastest. This basically kept speeds to a reasonable pace until that burning desire for something faster got the best of the racer, and the modifications began.

Mild modifications to the cars and engines were the norm, considering their dual use on the street and the drag strip. But it wasn't long before the need for speed demanded much more. Higher horsepower, lighter weight, and more traction were all elements leading the way to the purpose-built drag-racing machine.

Oh, what a time it was, that period of drag racing from the late 1940s through the 1960s. There was so much innovation and creativity that every time you went to a racetrack, you saw something radically new and different. Nothing was taboo and there were no rules limiting imagination, only some minimum criteria put in place to protect the racer from himself. Drag racing was created as a sport to get the action off the street and onto the much safer and organized drag strip. The pace of change in drag racing was accelerating as fast as one of the highly modified dragsters of the times.

What the racers lacked in sophistication, they replaced with enthusiastic creativity. They created machines with two wheels, three wheels, four wheels, six wheels, multiple engines, aircraft powerplants, multiwheel drive, and streamlining. Racers built exotic creations that bore little resemblance to the coupes and roadsters that represented the speed machines of the earliest days. All these vehicles and more had their day on the racetrack. Of course, some were not successful. But that did not prevent anyone from trying to be just a little bit better, quicker, and faster to the finish line than his competitor.

It was during this period of rapid growth and constant change that the legends of today were born—Garlits, the Bean Bandits, Karamasines, Postoian, the Chrismans, Mickey Thompson, Ivo, Prudhomme, Robinson, Arfons, Muldowney, Rice, and McEwen. These are just a few of the drivers whose names and accomplishments were recognized nationwide. Some of these greats are still active in the sport today.

Fueling the great leaps in performance as much as the car builders were the manufacturers building speed components. Their names formed a Who's Who in racing products: Edelbrock, Iskenderian, Donovan, Smith, Winfield, Pink, Engle, Weiand, Herbert, Black, and Milodon. The full list would contain hundreds of names of individuals and companies who were at the forefront of product development, allowing unbelievable increases in performance.

The manufacturers, car builders, drivers, tracks, and organizations went hand in hand—all attempting to keep pace with the explosion of speed that drag racing had become. From its earliest days in the 1940s—with speeds barely topping 100 miles per hour from a standing start in the quarter-mile—to the end of the 1960s—and a blast of over 238 miles per hour—drag racing displayed a growth in performance and excitement that built it into one of the world's top motorsports attractions. Today, as we continue into the twenty-first century, speeds topping 320 miles per hour in the same quarter-mile distance have become the standard of excellence for the nitromethane-powered categories.

By the end of the 1960s, the wild swings in creative genius in dragster design had evolved into a period of refinement. The racer was working to develop what had become a standard type of car, the front-engine dragster; every effort pointed toward finding that last bit of performance which would provide an advantage over the other guy. As the decade of the 1970s began, the dragsters were fighting for popularity with the newest drag-racing creation, the Funny Car, a vehicle that attracted strong brand loyalty due to its full-bodied design that looked, at that time, amazingly similar to the production line car. This Dragster vs. Funny Car battle continues today.

Little did the dragster racer of the late 1960s know that in just a few short years the face of drag racing would once again totally change with the creation of a successful rear or midengine design. But that's a story for another time.

Since that day in 1959, I have had the pleasure of working in the world of drag racing, announcing events both large and small all over the country. I feel like the luckiest man in the world, having a chance to make a living doing something I have done many times, just for fun. It has given me an opportunity to realize my dreams, to meet and work with some of the greatest people in the world, and to live through an era that will never be duplicated.

The sport of drag racing was created in the United States by the driving force of the youth of America, caught up in a competitive spirit that matches any sporting activity. The dedication of time and money is staggering, yet hundreds of thousands of America's youth have used drag racing as a springboard to success. This book will give you a glimpse into the life and times of drag racing in its most innovative and creative period. Some call it the Good Old Days. I look upon those decades as the time of our lives in drag racing. Enjoy and remember.

—*Dave McClelland*

In drag racing's short half-century history, the exact date, time, and location of the very first drag race was unfortunately never recorded. The origin of the term "drag" race is also unknown. What is known, however, is that the first *organized* drag race was in 1949 at the Goleta Air Base near Santa Barbara, California. The first runs there were experimental in nature. The cars ran approximately a quarter-mile. This was the distance from the starting line to a little ridge the cars bumped over, down the track, at which point they could determine who was the winner. But after a few meets, the facility was closed. Also in 1949, three other Southern California drag strips opened, but with only moderate success.

In the late 1940s, street racing had become a problem in Los Angeles. This coincided with a tremendous growth in the popularity of dry lakes racing. The emerging speed equipment industry was fanning the fires of competition by building specialized components for serious dry lakes competitors. Then came Bonneville's speed trials. By 1950 the average hot rodder had been aced out of contention by nitro-burning all-out race cars. The semiprofessionalism of the lakes racers left many grass roots hot rodders with no place to run except on the streets. And street racing was as convenient as the nearest intersection; no long hikes to the dry lake with the extra cost of an overnight stay.

Outside California, the problem was even worse. There were no dry lakes to run on, so the street became the only alternative for competition. And a new innovation from Detroit—the overhead valve engine—gave drivers with the money for a new car a machine that was every bit as quick as many of the flathead-powered homebuilt hot rods. These folks were also looking for a place to race.

By 1950 the demand for drag racing facilities was growing—especially in Southern California. By the end of that year, there were 5 drag strips in the Los Angeles area. In 1951 those facilities continued to thrive and 4 new strips opened in other states. In 1952 the number of strips in Southern California grew to 6, and out-of-state strips numbered 10. It was at this juncture that Wally Parks, then editor of *Hot Rod* magazine, formed the National Hot Rod Association. "We, *Hot Rod* magazine and SCTA [Southern California Timing Association], ran an experimental drag race at the blimp base in Orange County," recalls Parks. "Little by little, other tracks began to open." Pomona became the cornerstone of drag racing, because of the cooperation from local civic authorities. "Pomona had a police chief and a police department who were very much tuned in to providing activities to try to curtail street racing in their territory," says Parks. "So consequently, we had access to the LA Fairgrounds starting in 1950." This access continues today with the annual NHRA Winternationals and World Finals.

In addition to the NHRA, other sanctioning bodies fostered the growth of the fledgling sport. With the exception of the IHRA (International Hot Rod Association), the others (which included a short stint by NASCAR) have long since discontinued operations. The NHRA always maintained its focus on safety. Its founding motto was "Dedicated to Safety." "We realized at the time, if it couldn't be safe, it couldn't last," says Parks. This philosophy caused an uproar when the NHRA banned the use of exotic fuel in 1957. Even without special fuels, the NHRA continued to grow and keep up with the pace of the competitors' innovations. Competition class structure continually changed as car and engine technology evolved. "We didn't want to suppress development," says Parks. "But we were always trying to cultivate the sport to accommodate mass participation. We always wanted to keep it so anyone could get involved in any class in which they wanted to compete."

Throughout the 1950s and 1960s, drag racing experienced phenomenal growth, with drag strips popping up all across the nation. At the same time, the cost of horsepower was decreasing. The aftermarket industry was churning out hop-up parts and Detroit's manufacturers were gearing up for a horsepower war. It was the right time and place for drag racing.

From those early days, drag racing grew at an unbelievable rate. By 1955, NHRA sanctioned 68 drag strips in 31 states, with probably as many or more unsanctioned strips across the nation. Those NHRA facilities ran 434 events in 1955, drawing 565,741 spectators with 35,611 competition entries. At the dawn of the twenty-first century, NHRA's yearly attendance is approximately 2.5 million with millions more watching on television.

During the 50 years that the sport has been around, however, some things remain unchanged. The quarter-mile is still 1,320 feet long. The cars still begin the race from a standing start and the first car to the finish line is still the winner. Burning rubber still smells the same. The bark from open exhaust headers on a V-8 engine at full throttle still sounds the same. And the intense human desire to compete and win is still there. Along with that intense desire to win is a brotherly camaraderie between competitors, which has always been part of the sport.

The history of drag racing is about development of cars and engines of all types, and that consistent quarter-mile of pavement. These simple ingredients have created bonds between competitors and fans that endure to this day.

Most early drag strips were former World War II airfields. Paradise Mesa in San Diego, California, was one of those that opened in the early 1950s. Here a Studebaker makes a single run while other cars wait in the staging lanes. There were no bleachers for the spectators, so they simply lined the sides of the strip. *Don Cox*

Gas Dragsters

I f you had a dragster and wanted to compete at an NHRA-sanctioned event or an NHRA track between 1957 and 1963, you had to burn pump gas. The NHRA and a few selected race tracks had banned the use of exotic fuels. This was done to tame the sudden increases in speed these high-powered fuels produced. Many tracks were not long enough to allow cars to slow down and stop safely once they reached higher speeds. Also, many of the competitors' cars did not have the braking ability to handle the increased speed that nitro gave them. Without the extra horsepower exotic fuels produce, the competitors who remained and ran gas relied on their ingenuity. Twin engine dragsters soon appeared and the single engine dragster designs were refined. More competitors looked to supercharging for additional horsepower.

Gas Dragsters, especially unblown ones, were inexpensive and served as a great training ground for those who wanted to move into the dragster ranks. Tommy "The Watchdog" Allen, who would later go on to drive Fuel Dragsters, graduated from a Corvette up to an injected small-block Chevy Gas Dragster. Allen was only 20 years old at the time and simply wanted to go faster. In the early 1960s, he and a partner bought a Chassis Research frame and installed the 327 engine from his Corvette. Allen was helped in the transition from the Corvette to the dragster by Leonard Abbott, inventor of the Lenco transmission. "Abbott was a very poor drag racer who barely had enough money to get to the track," says Allen. "He built numerous race cars, from a dual-engine Chevy dragster to Top Fuel cars. He had a lot of ideas, and 60 percent of them didn't work. But one did—the transmission." To the youthful Allen, Abbott had the stature of a professional drag racer. Abbott helped him get the car to run and even drove it a few times. "He was a really great guy," recalls Allen.

Phil Parker of Odessa, Texas, owned this Chevy-powered A/Dragster. At the 1964 U.S. Nationals, it set the elapsed time record for its class at 8.95 seconds. The dragster's chassis was built by Dragmaster, a company started by Jim Nelson and Dode Martin. Pooling their talents and money, these two hard-core racers turned Dragmaster into the most successful chassis company of the Gas Dragster era.

Allen added a Hilborn injector to the 327 engine in his dragster. It was backed by a Cad LaSalle transmission and an early Ford rear end. The transmission only had second and third gear. "You could step on it pretty hard off the line," says Allen. "You couldn't just floor the thing, because it would just spin the tires." Once the dragster's combination was sorted out, Allen raced as much as he could. "We were maniacs! We'd go wherever there was a race." Allen's dragster would consistently run in the high 9- or low 10-second range at 145 miles per hour. This put his dragster in the same speed and elapsed time range as the A/Gas Supercharged coupes that were extremely popular at that time, and they were quite often matched up on the track. "In the two years that we ran that car, we raced every name that you can think of that had an A/Gas Supercharged

coupe—we never lost one time—not once," chirped Allen. The A/Gas cars would consistently qualify in the mid-9 second range, much quicker than Allen's dragster. But, the gassers had a hard time running those times consistently. "Those gassers were temperamental and you never knew what would happen," says Allen. "They hated to see us coming. They'd say, 'Here come those guys from San Diego with that little rotten dragster.' It was pretty funny."

Part of Allen's success came from his dragster's simplicity. Once he found a good combination, he didn't change it. "We were the last of the nontinkerers, and that was part of our success," says Allen. Through Leonard Abbott, Allen got to know Bruce Crower and Byron Blair, both of whom were in the high performance parts business and heavily involved in drag racing.

In 1959, Ivo was talked into running a blower on his Buick dragster—a modification he felt reduced the engine's reliability. Soon after this photo was taken, he parked this single-engine car for his new twin-engine dragster. *Tommy Ivo collection*

In 1958, Tommy Ivo raced his first dragster. It featured a gas-burning Buick engine in a Kent Fuller chassis. Ivo designed the exhaust pipes to run parallel to the front bars on the roll cage. *Tommy Ivo collection*

At the 1960 U.S. Nationals, the Trotters Hot Rod club from Columbus, Ohio, won best appearing car and crew. Their finely detailed B/Dragster was built on an Eliminator II chassis with a 96-inch wheelbase. The 1955 Chrysler engine had a Potvin cam and fuel injection. *James Genat/Zone Five Photo*

Leaving the line with a wisp of smoke from the rear tires is Tom Allen in his red B/Dragster. The 327 Chevy engine powering his car came directly from a Corvette he had previously raced. Backing the Corvette engine was a Cad/LaSalle transmission. Only second and high gears were used. *Tom Allen*

"Those guys wanted to experiment all the time—they wanted to keep going faster and faster. Even though half of their ideas didn't work, some of them did." Allen was satisfied with the car the way it was because it was a consistent winner. Eventually Allen gave in to the seduction of more speed. Instead of adding a blower to his Chevy, he decided to build a new dragster that would run in the A/Gas Dragster class. "They looked exactly like Top Fuel cars, but ran on gasoline instead of nitro," says Allen. "I was going to run gasoline because I couldn't afford nitro." In 1963, Allen went to Race Cars Specialties and ordered a new chassis. By the time Allen had his chassis, he was out of money and couldn't afford an engine. Don and Guy Cope were

brothers who had been involved in racing in the San Diego area. They approached Allen about running a blown Chrysler in his chassis, except they wanted to run on nitro. Once Allen had a ride in a fuel burner, he would never go back to gas.

One of the most successful Gas Dragsters ever built was the *Albertson Olds*. It was owned by two pioneers in drag racing, Gene Adams and Ronnie Scrima. Driving was Leonard Harris, who also brought the sponsorship from the Alberston Oldsmobile dealership. Harris was highly respected in Southern California drag racing circles for his driving ability.

Adams and Scrima selected a Chassis Research K-88 frame. Chassis Research, owned by Scotty Fenn, produced

The engine in the *Albertson Olds* was a bored and stroked Olds displacing 462 ci. It had a 671 GMC blower and fuel injection. Noticeably absent from the rear of the car is a drag chute, a safety item that was available but not yet required on dragsters.

For competition in the Gas Dragster class, many competitors constructed their own frames. Many of these early builders took their design cues from the established chassis manufacturers. This particular dragster, which was found a few years ago in the back of a bowling alley, has a frame design similar to those built by Chassis Research.

ready-to-race dragster frames. Fenn's designs were noted for their strength and short wheelbase. The frame under the *Albertson Olds* dragster had a 92-inch wheelbase. It was Fenn's theory that the wheelbase should not be any longer than the circumference of the rear tire.

In the early 1960s, Gas Dragster racers shied away from the Chrysler Hemi engine—they felt it was best run on nitro. The *Albertson Olds* was powered by a wedge head Oldsmobile engine, built by Gene Adams, that was bored and stroked to 462 ci. It featured an Engel cam, a GMC 671 blower, and Hilborn injectors. During the summer of 1960, with Harris at the helm,

the *Albertson Olds* took Southern California by storm. At Lions Drag Strip, it was victorious in 12 consecutive Saturday night shows. On Sundays, the Albertson team took its blue dragster to one of the other local drag strips and continued to fine-tune the combination.

Like so many other drag racers, Leonard Harris learned his driving skills on the streets of Los Angeles. When he drove the *Albertson Olds*, Harris sat low in the seat with his right hand at the 12 o'clock position on top of the butterfly steering wheel. His head was cocked to the left as he looked around the blower. Harris was a crafty driver who was often the first off the line. A typical dragster run in 1960 included clouds of smoke from the slicks, as the driver slid his left foot off the clutch at the start. Harris developed a technique of slipping the clutch just enough to avoid smoking the tires. This technique produced some very quick elapsed times and won many races.

At the end of a successful summer in Southern California, the *Albertson Olds* team trekked to Detroit, Michigan, for the 1960 NHRA U.S. Nationals. Twin-engine dragsters were the rage in 1960, and everyone predicted a Top Eliminator win by one of the many top teams running them. Southern California's Dragmaster team of Dode Martin and Jim Nelson quickly established themselves as favorites, when they set the fast speed of the meet at 171 miles per hour in their *Two Thing*. Martin and Nelson won the AA/Dragster class eliminations and were the favorites for Monday's Top Eliminator run-offs.

The *Albertson Olds* was one of 36 cars entered in the tough A/Dragster class. When the class eliminations were over, the winner was the *Albertson Olds*. On Monday, the first round for Top Eliminator saw the *Albertson Olds* against the Dragmaster *Two Thing*, with Harris beating the twin-engine Chevy dragster by a slim margin. Next, Harris would have to face Ray Godman's A/Modified Roadster *Tennessee Bo-Weevil*, for the title. Godman's blown Chrysler-powered roadster had handily won the A/Modified Roadster class during eliminations and set a national record of 9.97 seconds at 153.84 miles per hour. In the finals, Harris drove the *Albertson Olds* to the title. The 1960 NHRA Top Eliminator win earned the team a new 1960 Ford station wagon presented by the D-A Lubricant company. The Albertson team also won the *Motor Life* magazine award for best elapsed time at 9.25 seconds.

It looked like the *Albertson Olds* would never be beaten, as the team picked up where it left off at Lions Drag Strip. On September 24, the *Albertson Olds* dipped into the 8s with a pass

GREAT DRAG-RACING ENGINES: Chevrolet Small-Block V-8

Soon after making its appearance in 1955, the Chevy small-block engine quickly became a favorite of drag racers. It was lightweight, compact, easily modified, and revved like a kitchen blender. The small-block Chevy engine was used extensively in Gas Dragsters, Gas Coupes and Roadsters, Production and Modified Sports Cars, and Altereds.

In the spring of 1952, Ed Cole became Chevrolet's chief engineer. It was his job to breathe life into what had become a stodgy car line that was losing sales. Within a short time, Cole expanded Chevrolet's engineering staff from 851 to 2,900 people. He also proposed a new engine for the Chevrolet. His experience with General Motors' military tank division and Cadillac prepared him for one of the greatest achievements of his life—the small-block Chevy engine.

Cole, along with Chevrolet engineering whiz Harry Barr, set strict parameters for the new engine's design. Because of the high volume of vehicles built by Chevrolet, the new engine had to be inexpensive to manufacture and easy to assemble. It also had to operate efficiently for the consumer. Cole decided that the displacement should be 265 ci (3.75 bore and 3.00 stroke). The cylinder heads were designed to be interchangeable and cast with integral valve guides. The intake manifold also acted as the valley cover and provided a common water outlet for both heads. One of the keys to the engine's simplicity was the valvetrain. Stamped rocker arms were retained by a fulcrum ball and lock nut on a pressed-in stud. Oiling for the valvetrain was through hollow pushrods, which saved the complexity of external oil feeder lines. New techniques devised for casting the blocks provided for a more accurate bore placement. The new engine weighed 41 pounds less than the Blue Flame six.

The new 265-ci V-8, with horsepower ratings of 162 and 180, was released in the completely restyled 1955 Chevy. Forty-three percent of all new 1955 Chevrolets were V-8 optioned. Before the first full tank of gas had run through a production Chevy equipped with a V-8, aftermarket suppliers were tooling up for speed components. Up until 1955, the only V-8s with any potential were the newer overhead valve Cadillac and Oldsmobile V-8s, which were heavy and expensive. Prior to their release, the Ford flathead was the only V-8 game in town. While plentiful, the flathead's horsepower peak had been attained. The 265 Chevy's initial low cost and high horsepower potential encouraged competitors to begin installing them in race cars of all types.

In 1956, Chevrolet added a dual quad option and the horsepower jumped to 225. The following year, the company bumped displacement up to 283 and added fuel injection. These changes allowed Chevy's little V-8 to reach the magical one-horsepower-per-cubic-inch mark. By 1961 the 283 was pumping out an amazing 315 horsepower. Just when small-block lovers felt it couldn't get any better, Chevrolet increased the displacement to 327 ci in 1962. Chevrolet's ongoing development of the small block meant an inexpensive hot cam or aluminum intake manifold was as close as the nearest Chevy dealer's parts department. For additional power, aftermarket cams, intake manifolds, and fuel injection units were available.

The NHRA fuel ban just happened to coincide with the release of the 283. Those racers who continued to run Gas Dragsters found the small-block Chevy to be the ideal powerplant. The new little Chevy engine easily lent itself to boring and stroking for additional cubic inches. It responded to traditional hop-up techniques, and was also very amenable to supercharging. Pound for pound and dollar for dollar, the small-block Chevy has been one of the drag racer's favorite engines for nearly 50 years.

The *Dragmaster Dart* was one of the most famous of the Dragmaster-built cars. Driven by both Jim Nelson and Dode Martin, it was a consistent winner in the AA/Dragster class. Its most celebrated win was Top Eliminator at the 1962 Winternationals. It was built out of lightweight chrome moly tubing and weighed only 1,250 pounds.

The advertisement for Inyokern Drag Strip's NHRA record runs featured the *Dragmaster Dart*. Also shown in this ad is the *Starlight*, a Chrysler-powered Dragmaster-chassised car that ran nitro. A Dragmaster chassis with a Hemi, especially a fuel-burning Hemi, was rare.

of 8.96 seconds at a speed of 171.42 miles per hour. A match race was scheduled for October 22, 1960, between the *Albertson Olds* and Howard Johansen's twin-Chevy-powered dragster. Although billed by Lions Drag Strip promoters as the "Match Race of the Century," it never materialized. Both dragsters were sidelined with mechanical problems. During a tune-up run, the twin Chevy blew one of its engines. Harris made a single run in the *Albertson Olds*, after which water began running out of the engine from a cracked head. The smell of bad luck seemed to be in the air, but Harris didn't notice. He took the opportunity to drive the new *Firestone Realty* dragster. In the first round of

The *Dragmaster Dart* was powered by a 426-ci Dodge engine. The GMC 671 supercharger was fed by a Hilborn injector. Horsepower on gasoline was estimated to be 750.

paid their dues racing on Southern California's dry lake beds. In 1957 they teamed up to build their first dragster, the *Dragliner*. At the 1957 NHRA Nationals in Oklahoma City, it ran the quarter in 10.30 seconds at a speed of 135 miles per hour, taking C/Dragster honors. By 1959 they had the basic design completed for what would be their bread-and-butter chassis. The quality of workmanship in that car attracted other racers, who asked them for a complete new chassis or other dragster components. Initially Martin worked in the racing shop full-time, while Nelson worked a "real job." Soon the volume of work demanded his undivided attention, too.

Following experiments with the *Two Thing* twin-engine dragster, Martin and Nelson settled on what would become their signature chassis—the Dragmaster. It was a sturdy, no-frills design that was highly distinguishable from the other manufactured dragster chassis available. "We started out with the first little model similar to the one on the *Mooneyes* dragster that we called the Mark I," says Martin. The Mark I had a 96-inch wheelbase and was quickly followed by the Mark II, which had a 98-inch wheelbase. "Then we went to a model we called the Straight Arrow. The last model was the Dart chassis; it was a little more streamlined," Martin says. The Dart also had a longer 124-inch wheelbase.

To the untrained eye, it's difficult to discern that a bare dragster chassis is, in fact, a race car. This came to light when Martin and Nelson were on their way to a race in Texas. In addition to towing their race car, they also had a bare chassis (for a customer) strapped to the roof of their old Chrysler station wagon. "We were driving across Texas at about 80 miles an hour," recalls Martin. "When the police stopped us, the officer said with a heavy Texas accent, 'My name is Mr. Wyatt. Why you all going so fast?' I explained we were going to the races. He didn't give us a ticket, but he did ask why we had a dog sled tied to the roof of the car! I said, man, that's no dog sled—it's a race car!"

By 1962 the Dragmaster chassis was the one to have. Its simple, functional design was loved by top racers such as Pete Robinson (1961 Nationals winner), Roland Leong, and Mickey Thompson (1962 Nationals winner with Jack Chrisman driving). While usually seen with a small-block Chevy between the rails, the Dragmaster chassis would accept almost any type of engine. Each chassis was also tailored to fit the physique of the driver who ordered it. Steering wheel and pedals were positioned for driver comfort and convenience. Dragmaster would

eliminations, the steering failed and the dragster flipped. Harris was killed. Because of his exceptional driving ability, Harris almost surely would have become the first nationally recognized star in drag racing, had he not died at the wheel.

Another notable chassis manufacturer of the early 1960s was Dragmaster, located in Carlsbad, California. Dragmaster was owned by Dode Martin and Jim Nelson. They produced one of the nicest ready-to-race dragster chassis available. In addition to building dragster chassis for many competitors, they also raced one of their own chassis. Both Martin and Nelson

Dean Moon was the owner of the Moon Equipment Company, an aftermarket supplier to the hot rod industry. His trademark "Moon Eyes" was painted on everything he owned and *Mooneyes* was also the name of his A/Gas Dragster. His dragster was a rolling test bed for his products and the products of his suppliers.

even make the roll cage larger for those who needed it. Between 200 and 300 Dragmaster chassis were built.

One of the most famous Dragmaster chassised dragsters was Martin and Nelson's *Dragmaster Dart*—the gold and red-trimmed Dodge-powered dragster that was Top Eliminator at the 1962 Winternationals. What better way to showcase the products your company builds than by using them in competi-

tion. And, what better way to demonstrate the quality of your product than by winning one of the biggest races of the year.

The *Dragmaster Dart* weighed in at 1,250 pounds, which was about the same weight as Pete Robinson's small-block Chevy-powered Dragmaster dragster. The *Dragmaster Dart* was a standard Dragmaster chassis, except it was made out of .028 wall lightweight chrome moly tubing. It, like all of the

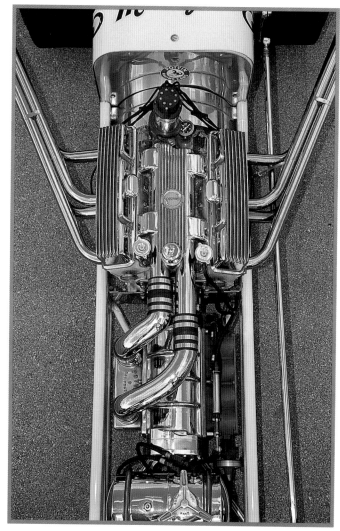

ABOVE:

The *Mooneyes'* Dragmaster chassis featured the optional double rollbar. The high seating position and crankshaft-driven blower gave the driver an excellent view of the track. In 1962 the *Mooneyes* dragster was the first dragster to win both of NHRA's big events—the Winternationals and the U.S. Nationals. It also was shipped to England, where it made exhibition runs.

TOP:

Mooneyes was built on the early Mark I Dragmaster chassis. It was powered by a 301-ci Chevy with a crankshaft-driven blower. On its very first run, it clocked a speed of 147 miles per hour.

RIGHT:

Dean Moon cleared his parts shelf when he outfitted his *Mooneyes* dragster. The finned valve covers were a Moon product, and the Potvin crankshaft blower drive was a component that he sold, along with the famous Moon fuel tank.

Vern Tratechaud designed and built his own dragster, which he ran in the B/Dragster class. Named *Touché*, it was powered by a fuel-injected 301-ci Chevy. At the 1960 U.S. Nationals, he set the NHRA National Record for speed, at 142.63 miles per hour. The overall design had a very low profile and ground clearance was at a minimum.

Driving a dragster can be a hair-raising adventure. Here, Vern Tradechaud's *Touché* dragster raises the front wheels off of the line. A quick start meant finding the balance between bogging, doing a wheelstand, or smoking the tires. *Vern Tratechaud collection*

Dragmaster chassis, was welded with an acetylene torch with stainless rod. Martin and Nelson saved additional weight by using a single disc brake on the left rear wheel. The Dragmaster wheelbase was 124 inches with an overall length of 167 inches. The height at the rollbar was 45 inches and its ground clearance was 3.7 inches.

The *Dragmaster Dart* was unusual in that it ran a Dodge engine, while most competitors in AA/Dragster class were using Chevys. Dodge and Plymouth Super Stocks had been tearing up the track with their wedge head engine, but this engine had gone virtually unnoticed by competitors in other classes. Nelson and Martin selected a 383-ci block as a starting point. That block had the largest bore (4.25 inches) of any of the wedge blocks. To the 383 block, they married a crankshaft with a 3.75 stroke from a 413 wedge engine. This gave them an engine with a total displacement

FLAGMAN

Long before there was a Christmas Tree starting system, a human being stood out in front of the cars and started the race with a green flag. Most flagmen developed a style that added a certain amount of showmanship to each race. *Greg Sharp collection*

Up until 1963, almost all drag races were started by a flagman. The cars would be brought up to the starting line with the aid of two assistants, one assigned to each lane. These assistants would check the car and the driver for safety equipment. The assistant would motion the driver forward, placing the front tires inches behind the starting line beams. At that point, it would be up to the flagman, positioned 20 feet ahead of the cars in the center of the track. In his hands were two flags, one red and the other green. Once the cars were in position and the track was clear behind him, the starter would place the tip of the green flag on the racing surface directly in front of him. Then he would point the red flag at each driver, looking for a nod to indicate that they were ready. When he lifted the green flag off of the track—the race was on. If one of the competitors moved before he raised the flag, the starter would wave the red flag indicating a foul start, and the cars would back up and try it again.

Veteran drivers learned to study each flagman for little idiosyncrasies that telegraphed when he was going to lift the flag. "Big Daddy" Don Garlits always concentrated on the starter's bicep. When he saw it tighten—he dropped the clutch. "Dyno" Don Nicholson was often called a flag jumper because he was so quick off the line. He loved flagmen who were more theatrical in their approach to raising the flag. Many would look away just before raising the flag to try and fake-out the drivers. These flagmen had no idea if someone jumped or not and Nicholson regularly took advantage of them—and the competition.

As with most jobs at early drag strips, the starter's position was filled by a member of the track's crew, who also had other duties. Dave Crane flagged cars at Martin Drag Strip in Martin, Michigan. "In May of 1962, I started to work there running the scales. I was teching-in what we called the 'wire wheel' cars [Altereds and Dragsters]." Crane and the other crew members shared the flagging responsibilities. "No one taught me how to flag, they just handed the flags to me. I loved the job—I couldn't get close enough to the cars," giggled Crane. "I'd come home on Sunday night and I couldn't hear anything—just the ringing of the motors in my head. I didn't wear ear plugs; we were young and going to live forever. You never thought about things like that."

One of Crane's best memories as a flagman was when he started a match race between Bobby Walters' fuel dragster and Nook Bakewell in Art Arfrons' jet. "The regular starter didn't want to get out there," recalls Crane. "We had the dragster in the right lane and the jet in the left lane. I stood in the grass on the right side by the dragster." Prior to the first run, Bakewell took Crane aside and gave him some final instructions. "He told me, 'You point the flag at me and I'll nod. You point the flag at Bobby Walters and he nods. When you put that flag on the ground, you count one-thousand one, one-thousand two and you lift the flag— because when that flag first hits the ground—I'm leaving.' " Bakewell's two-second-delay starting instructions were given to compensate for the delay in the jet engine's spool-up time. "Those cars came off absolutely side by side," says Crane with an ear-to-ear smile. "What a sight—here I am, right next to the track in the best seat in the house. I turned around and Bobby Walters was going away from me in a cloud of tire smoke and Bakewell's jet going away in a ball of fire. It sent chills down my spine!"

In 1963 the "Christmas tree" starting system was introduced, and the flagmen's green and red flags were traded in for a small electrical box with a toggle switch. Now called the "starter," he stands back and flips a switch to activate the tree. It's a lot less colorful than watching the man jumping in the air waving a flag, but it's a system that's fairer to the racers and can provide a handicapped start.

INSET:
Garlits' *Swamp Rat IV* used a supercharged wedge 413 Dodge engine. In 1962 most racers believed that the Chrysler Hemi engine was not suitable for gasoline-burning dragsters. Most of the successful teams ran engines with wedge-style combustion chambers.

Don Garlits built only one dragster specifically for racing on gasoline—the *Swamp Rat IV*. It had a 120-inch wheelbase (slightly longer than most of its competition) and was constructed of lightweight material, similar to other gas-burning dragsters of the era. Garlits took this car to the 1962 U.S. Nationals but lost to Mickey Thompson in the final round.

of 426 ci, without having to buy an expensive stroker crank. The heads were reworked and used stock valves that had been lightened. The cam was an Isky roller grind with a relatively mild profile. This allowed power to be built over a wider rpm range.

On top of the engine was a 671 supercharger driven at 1.22 times crank speed. The fuel injection unit was a Hilborn. Because of its compact size, a Mallory Mini-Mag magneto was used. Nelson and Martin estimated that the engine put out about 750 horsepower.

On the car's first outing, the *Dart* ran a respectable 160 miles per hour in the quarter. But it wasn't without its teething problems. As the car neared the traps, driver Nelson spotted flames licking out of the exhaust pipes. It turned out that the roller lifters were rising out of their bores as engine speeds increased, causing valve float. This also restricted oil flow to the bearings, causing the bearings to fail. A set of helper springs were added, which applied pressure to the tops of the lifters, keeping them in their bores. Problem solved!

In addition to winning the 1962 Winternationals, the *Dragmaster Dart* also won NHRA's Southeastern Divisional drags, held in Memphis, Tennessee. There, the Martin and Nelson duo (both drove the car) outran everyone in the AA/Dragster class and set both ends of the national record, running 8.63 seconds at 176.12 miles an hour.

Mickey Thompson owned the Dragmaster-chassised AA/Dragster that Jack Chrisman drove to the winner's circle at the 1962 U.S. Nationals. This car was much different from the *Dragmaster Dart*. The era of the short-wheelbase dragsters was coming to an end, and Chrisman's stretched 128-inch wheelbase was a prime example of the future look of dragster chassis. Chrisman's car was also extremely light. When it weighed in at 1,090 pounds, it was 63 pounds under the AA/Dragster class minimum. To make the class requirements, a lead-filled bar was mounted 6 inches forward of the front axle. One reason for Chrisman's dragster's feather-like weight was its all-aluminum Pontiac V-8. Thompson had connections within Pontiac and was able to obtain an experimental aluminum 389-ci cylinder block. With the addition of a stroker crankshaft, the total displacement grew to 432 ci. Thompson added a set of specially constructed hemispherical aluminum heads. These heads looked like Chrysler Hemi heads and worked as well. The combination of an excellent chassis, a powerful lightweight engine, and superb driving ability made Chrisman unbeatable, as he took Top Eliminator honors. In addition, he set low elapsed time of the meet at 8.60 seconds.

While Kent Fuller was most famous for building nitro-burning dragsters, he also made a few raced on gas. The beautiful *Western Manufacturing Special* ran a blown Chevy engine wrapped in an Arnie Roberts aluminum body. This dragster has all the classic lines of the larger fuel dragsters of the era.

One of Dragmaster's earliest customers was Dean Moon. He built his *Mooneyes* B/Gas Dragster using a Dragmaster Mark I design chassis. It was powered by a 301-ci small-block Chevy with a crankshaft-driven GMC 671 blower. One of the small-block Chevy's best weapons was rpm, and Moon's little dragster used every one to its advantage. With a rear-end ratio of 4.68 (quite high for a dragster), it was designed to launch at 9,000 rpm. That was also the rpm it would be taching through the traps. The bright yellow *Mooneyes* dragster was a rolling advertisement for Moon's parts business. Some of the items that Moon built and sold on the car were his "no-name" valve covers, fuel tank, valve cover breathers, and hydraulic throttle linkage. Moon's dragster was also a great place to test other manufacturers' parts that he sold, such as the Potvin intake and blower drive.

The first time out, *Mooneyes* ran 147 miles an hour with an elapsed time of 10.29 seconds. Dean Moon was one of the car's first drivers, followed by Dragmaster's Jim Nelson and Gary Cagle. When Cagle drove it at the 1962 Winternationals, it ran 153.06 miles an hour with a 9.52-second elapsed time, good enough to win the A/Dragster class. The *Mooneyes* rail was the

Tony Nancy refers to his first dragster as the *Silver Car.* It was designed by Steve Swaja, seen on the left packing the drag chute. Swaja's design gave the *Silver Car* an unusual extended rear body. It was powered by a 482-ci Plymouth wedge engine. *Tony Nancy collection*

first dragster to garner a win at both of NHRA's premier events, the Winternationals and the U.S. Nationals. In 1963, *Mooneyes* was shipped to England for some exhibition runs. With Dante Duce at the wheel, it ran 164 miles per hour on a rough World War II airfield.

Phil Parker was another Dragmaster customer. He was from Odessa, Texas, and ran a Dragmaster chassis on his A/Dragster at the 1964 Winternationals, where it set the record of 8.95 seconds. Jess Van Deventer built the engine and occasionally drove the car. "This car drove like a dream," Van Deventer recalls of Parker's dragster. "All the Dragmaster cars were built great!" As *well* built as the Dragmaster chassis were, they didn't fit in with the new breed of nitro racer's needs. The Dragmaster star fell as quickly as it had risen, as those running fuel-burning Hemis looked to other chassis builders for their new cars. They no longer needed a lightweight chassis like the Dragmaster designed for a small Chevy engine. Heavier and longer chassis were required for the fuel-burning Chrysler Hemi engine's mass and horsepower. Once they saw that the future of dragsters was in the fuel class, Martin and Nelson decided to shut down their chassis business.

Jim Nelson and Dode Martin were two of the nicest guys in drag racing and while no longer building dragster chassis, they stayed in and around racing and ran their shop in Carlsbad well into the 1990s. "We were just out racing, trying to beat everyone," says Martin. "And then we'd tell everybody what we used to do—like which cam we had in the engine."

Many of the competitors who ran in the Gas Dragster class built their own chassis. Their designs took the best from the commercially available Dragmaster and

Tony Nancy's *Silver Car* maintained its position on the *Drag News* Top Ten list for two years. It's seen here at the 1963 NHRA Winternationals running without its nose piece. Like most competitors in the dragster ranks, Nancy soon moved to fuel-burning dragsters. *Tony Nancy collection*

Chassis Research frames. Vern Tratechaud, of Detroit, decided he could build a chassis that was as good as or better than any available at the time. By day, Tratechaud was a machinist and by night he studied mechanical engineering. He used both of these disciplines in the design and construction of his Chevy-powered B/Dragster.

Tratechaud's chassis resembled an early Chassis Research frame, with its exaggerated skid bar roll cage, but that's where the similarity ended. Tratechaud's 101-inch wheelbase chassis used the engine as a load-bearing member. This design reduced the overall weight of the car and offered a rigid center section. Tratechaud also designed and built the front axle, adjustable front torsion bars, and friction shocks. One of the most unusual features of his car was the forward-mounted 1946 Crosley steering box. It was placed there to reduce the length of the drag link. The traditional long drag links on dragsters had a tendency to whip at high speeds, causing stability problems. This design required the long steering shaft, which is nestled between the injectors and left-hand rocker cover. Clearance for the steering shaft required some artistic bends in the aluminum body, which was also built by Tratechaud.

Powering Tratechaud's B/Dragster was a 301-ci Chevy with Hilborn fuel injection. It was backed by a 1950 Packard transmission and a quick change rear end. At the 1960 NHRA U.S. Nationals in Detroit, Tratechaud's dragster set the speed record for B/Dragsters, at 142.63 miles per hour. The car was run through the 1967 season, winning trophies on the track and at car shows.

In 1962, Don Garlits joined the wedge head gas burners when he debuted his *Swamp Rat IV*. He designed this light-weight dragster, with a 120-inch wheelbase, around the 413-ci Dodge wedge engine. At that time, Garlits was also running a Dodge, with a 413 engine, in the Super Stock class. *Swamp Rat IV* was designed to run strictly on gas. Garlits took it to the 1962 NHRA U.S. Nationals, where he made it to the final round, only to be beaten by Mickey Thompson's Pontiac-powered dragster. The best time for the *Swamp Rat IV* was 7.82 seconds at 185 miles per hour. When it came time for a match race in 1962, Garlits raced the fuel-burning Hemi-powered *Swamp Rat III*.

In 1963, Tony Nancy debuted his first dragster. His three previous roadsters had graced the cover of *Hot Rod* magazine. Like them, Nancy's dragster was highly detailed and beautifully finished. He simply called it the *Silver Car*.

It had a beautiful, full body designed by Steve Swaja. The *Silver Car* was powered by a Plymouth 426-ci wedge engine that was stroked to a total of 482 ci. "It said Plymouth Super Stock down the nose," says Nancy. "That was my first help from the factory."

Steve Swaja was one of the best young automotive designers in the early 1960s. His technical illustrations filled the pages of automotive enthusiast magazines. The body he designed for Tony Nancy's *Silver Car* was unusual because of its extended rear body. This extension housed the drag chute. Swaja designed slots into the rear section to funnel air to the chute. The extended rear-end design made it look as though Nancy sat further back in the car than he actually did. "People would ask me, 'How can you see the drag strip?'" Nancy explained that onlookers' perceptions differed from his view in the driver seat. From there, he was looking around a blower anyway. Artfully hidden in the rear edge of the body, below the parachute opening, was an extended horizontal push bar. This push bar was crafted out of half-inch aluminum and was bolted to the rear of the chassis. Half-inch aluminum plate was also used for the rear motor mounting plate, which doubled as the firewall.

Nancy's *Silver Car* wore a full nose piece, which very few dragsters had at the time. Jim Summers was responsible for the aluminum bodywork and Dick Hallen applied the Cadillac silver paint. This nose piece provided a good space for the sponsor's name.

"It was an excellent running gas car," recalls Nancy. The *Silver Car* maintained a position on the *Drag News* Mr. Eliminator list for two years. "You had to race against somebody every 30 days. The person on the list who was challenged had his choice of which drag strip to run." Nancy would set up those match races at either Pomona or San Fernando. "That car was exceptionally successful for a gas car," he says. Nancy retired the *Silver Car* as nitromethane fuel became legal at NHRA meets, and he, like many other competitors, moved up into the nitro ranks.

Gas Dragsters continued to have their own class until 1971. Through the later years of the class, the Chrysler Hemi, once thought not to be practical as a Gas Dragster engine, became the most popular powerplant. Then, the overwhelming popularity of the nitro-burning Funny Cars and Fuel Dragsters relegated the Gas Dragsters to the history books. These fuel dragsters built upon the engine and chassis developments of the Gas Dragster era.

Top Fuel Dragsters

In every sport there is one undeniable premier class at the top of the hill that refuses to be pushed off. In drag racing, it's Top Fuel Dragsters. The light dragster chassis with its monster-cubic-inch supercharged fuel-burning engine tearing down the strip will make your eyes water, your ears ring, and every internal organ vibrate out of place. And that's just if you're a fan watching from the stands. Nitromethane makes Top Fuel Dragsters the loudest, quickest, and fastest of them all. Nitromethane turns boys into men in a few seconds, giving fans the excitement they came to see.

Early drag racers found that one of the ways they could increase horsepower in any engine was to increase the compression ratio. Unfortunately, the pump gas available at the time didn't have enough octane to prevent detonation with higher compression ratios. To fix this problem, drag racers adopted a fuel that had first been run in Indy cars in the 1930s—methanol (methyl alcohol). Methanol became the first widely accepted alternative fuel for drag racers. But drag racers have never been satisfied, so they experimented with fuel additives. These additives could be almost any combustible liquid, including hydrogen peroxide, benzene, benzol, acetone, diethel ether, and toluene, to name a few. And there were even some additives that came in a crystal form such as picric acid.

Racers settled on nitromethane as the most cost-effective power booster. Chemists knew nitromethane as CH_3NO_2. Racers knew of it as "pop" or just plain "nitro." Its strength and volatility are given away by the warning label on the various containers: *May detonate if sensitized by amines, alkalies, strong acids, high temperatures or adiabatic compression. The dry alkali or amine salts are shock-sensitive and the sodium salt ignites on contact with water. Incompatible with amines, strong acids, strong bases, strong oxidizing agents, strong reducing agents, copper, copper alloys, lead, lead alloys. Flammable. [Used as detonating agent, fuel, solvent, gasoline additive.]* Nitro can be lethal.

In the early 1960s, this was the one car and driver that no Top Fuel driver wanted to see in the lane next to him. The Greer-Black-Prudhomme dragster was the baddest of them all. Its Chrysler engine had a definite nose-down attitude that set a trend other builders soon followed. Laying down the power were 10-inch-wide American magnesium racing wheels mounting 10.00x16 M&H tires. The small scoop behind the driver was to help the deployment of the drag chute.

The first dragsters to hit the strip were merely a set of frame rails, an engine, and a little bodywork. The car in the near lane has both the driver and engine set back, with the remnants of a roadster body. The car in the far lane is a World War II belly tank that was most frequently seen on the dry lakes. *Joaquin Arnett collection*

This Blair's Speed Shop–sponsored dragster has a severely narrowed chassis and roadster body with an attractive heart-shaped grille insert. Its flathead engine has three two-barrel Stromberg carbs. *Joaquin Arnett collection*

To run gasoline efficiently in an internal combustion engine, it takes an air-to-fuel ratio of approximately 12:1. Increasing or decreasing the ratio of fuel to air will not make it run any better. In fact, increasing the ratio will produce a mixture so rich that it will not ignite because there will not be enough oxygen to support combustion. Nitromethane was an ideal fuel additive because it brings its own oxygen into the combustion chamber. Typically mixed with methanol, nitromethane provides excellent increases in volumetric efficiency in any internal combustion engine. Nitro provides the engine with substantially more oxygen, so much more that the air-to-fuel ratios can be as high as 1:1. The result is the more fuel the engine can ignite, the more power it can produce. A dramatic cooling of the incoming fuel charge also occurs with nitro because of the high ratio of liquid in the mixture. Fuel energy delivered to the combustion chamber is 2.3 times that of gasoline for the same mass of air. Nitro also offers a higher flame, and flame speed. A 50 percent blend of nitro in methanol increases the power output of the average internal combustion engine by 45 percent over pure methanol. Higher percentages increase the output even more. Nitro was pure lightning and thunder in a bottle.

Joaquin Arnett, of the Bean Bandits club in San Diego, California, was one of the early and frequent users of nitro. In the early 1950s, he had been racing his roadster on the street and at

These three young men are eyeballing the *Eyeball Special* dragster. Like most dragsters in 1954, its frame rails are from an earlier passenger car. The engine is a flathead with high-compression heads and three Stromberg carburetors. Covering the top of the carbs is a flash shield that prevents the air stream from siphoning gas out of the carbs at high speed. This car does not have a rollbar. The battery is mounted over the front spring mount. *Don Cox*

over to the nitromethane." Arnett also ran a small percentage of picric acid, a tri-ni-tro compound that is a flammable solid. In its normal state, picric acid is a fine, moist yellow powder. When dry, it becomes a powerful high explosive. "These other guys had no idea what I was running," says Arnett. "I only ran 1 or 2 percent. A lot of guys who tried it watched as their pistons passed the crank." Arnett ran against three of the Oilers' best cars and beat them all easily. He toyed with the first two competitors, letting them get a substantial lead before he opened it up to pass them. The third competitor was simply left in the dust. Arnett ran this same Model T roadster at Santa Ana's new drag strip, where it would run 90 to 100 miles per hour on gas. Nitro would boost the speed from 115 to 118. Arnett found that

Paradise Mesa drag strip. Jim Nelson (later of Dragmaster fame) challenged Arnett to bring his roadster up to a new dirt drag strip that had been laid out on the north side of the county in Carlsbad. Nelson wanted Arnett to run against some of the cars in a local club called the Oilers. Arnett told him, "I have a T-model that's more sophisticated than anything you've ever seen." The car Arnett was referring to was a flathead-powered full-fendered Model T roadster that he drove on the street and raced on the strip. The multicarbed flathead was a family affair. "My wife die-ground all the ports, while she and her girlfriends sat in the kitchen drinking coffee," Arnett recalls with a laugh.

Arnett accepted Nelson's challenge. He changed all the carburetors so they would accept his fuel mixture. "I took off the carbs and dumped the gas out of them and then I filled them with alcohol so it would start on pure alcohol—then I'd switch

Don Garlits may have perfected the rear engine dragster, but he didn't invent it. Rear engine (actually midengine) dragsters were not unusual in the mid-1950s. Like most hot cars in 1954, this one is running a flathead with headers that sweep back smoothly into collectors. The small rollbar would protect only the driver's shoulders in case of a rollover accident. There is a small belly pan, but no other bodywork on the car. On the rear is a large set of recap slicks and the pushbar is welded to the rear end's center section. *Don Cox*

In 1955, Duncan and Lonski raced this purple dragster. It was powered with a fuel-injected nitro-burning Chrysler Hemi engine. Here, it's being repositioned on the track as the starter, with green flag in hand, waits patiently. *Don Cox*

Most mid-1950s dragsters were built in a neighborhood garage by early motorheads, much like these two. This flathead-powered dragster has a sheet aluminum body stretched over a tube frame. The cylinder on the side of the cockpit is a hand-pump that provides pressure to the fuel tank. The seat and seat belt are surplus aircraft units. The rear tires are recap slicks and the front tires are from a farm implement. *Don Cox*

he liked drag racing much better than racing on the dry lake beds. "Drag racing was so much easier, cleaner, and not so far to go," says Arnett.

In 1950 the classification of cars at the drag strip followed what the SCTA had done at the lakes: Stock-Bodied Coupes, Roadsters, and Sedans and Racing Coupes, Roadsters, and Sedans. The racing versions were stripped of fenders and the racing roadsters ran without windshields. As racing intensified, drivers removed more body parts. The car that's usually identified as the first rail was Dick Kraft's *Bug*. It was merely a flathead-powered frame with a small cowl and a seat. In 1950 it ran 150 miles per hour.

By 1954 the cars built especially for drag racing were more sophisticated. They were now called "dragsters." The word "dragster" first appeared in the January 1953 issue of *Hot Rod* magazine when they described Art Chrisman's 25 car. Dragster bodies were narrower than a standard roadster and the driver sat in the center of the car, nearly over the rear axle. In October 1954, the Automobile Timing Association of America (ATAA) held its World Series of Drag Racing in Lawrence, Kansas. Held in the geographic center of the country, the event drew dragsters from across the nation.

The ATAA's goal was to bring together cars from the East and West for what it called a "Bonneville of the Drags." While most competitors were from the Midwest, Joaquin Arnett led his Bean Bandit contingent from the West Coast. They brought a beautiful yellow dragster that Arnett had built. It was so nice, Arnett won the ATAA award for engineering achievement. "I started seeing that you needed a longer car and I built a beautiful car," boasts a proud Arnett. "I made the nose out of aluminum and everybody was shocked when I got it together." The first engine in Arnett's dragster was a flathead, which he ran at the Lawrence, Kansas, meet. Behind the flathead was a manual transmission. The driver would start in second and shift to high. Unfortunately for Arnett and his fellow club members, they blew three transmissions in as many runs. In the only run that Arnett completed in the car, he turned 126 miles per hour. It was a high-gear-only run, in which two of the club members poured water on the rear tires at the starting line so they would spin. The final bit of bad luck was a broken rear axle.

Arnett continued to refine his dragster and eventually removed the carburated flathead in favor of an injected Ardun, and finally a carburated Chrysler Hemi. With those engines it ran a multidisc clutch with a direct drive. "That car went awful fast and it handled good—anybody could drive it," says Arnett. With this setup, the dragster hit speeds as high as 157 miles per hour. Arnett ran two different tires. "For top time [speed], we were running Indianapolis tires with a mag wheel," says Arnett. "We were also running a drag tire that was a vulcanized rubber recap. We started to narrow down the tire and let it smoke."

The last nitro-burning drag racer to win an NHRA national event was Melvin Heath of Rush Springs, Oklahoma. Heath had unsuccessfully raced at the two previous NHRA Championship meets. For the 1956 meet, Heath built a new car. He made his new dragster's frame out of steel tubing. Up front was a 1937 Ford front axle and the rear end was from a 1940 Ford. Heath built the sheet metal body himself. It was similar in design to the other dragsters running at the time. The rear of the

Behind the wheel of this dragster under construction is a young Joaquin Arnett. This car was quite advanced for 1953, with its tubular frame, overhead valve V-8, and custom-made aluminum body. *Joaquin Arnett collection*

Placing the driver behind the rear axle allowed for the engine to be located rearward in the chassis, improving traction. The name "slingshot" came about because of this driver placement. This 1955-era dragster is powered by a Chrysler Hemi engine. *Don Cox*

In 1955 the Pomona Valley Timing Association had one of the most beautiful dragsters in the country. Its red-and-white body was more like an Indy roadster than a dragster. Indy-style mag wheels and front tires were paired with slicks on the rear. *Joaquin Arnett collection*

body housed the fuel tank and was rounded similar to the sprint cars of the era. Heath sat high over the rear axle with a small rollbar for protection.

Heath spared no expense when it came to his Chrysler Hemi engine. It featured JE pistons, a Chet Herbert cam, and oversize valves. Six Stromberg 97 carburetors were mounted on a Crower U-FAB log intake manifold. (The Crower U-FAB manifold came as a kit that the purchaser had to weld together.) A 1939 Ford transmission transmitted power to the rear axle.

Prior to the 1956 Nationals, Heath's dragster won two important meets: the Southwest Regional at Caddo Mills, Texas, and the Missouri Valley Regional at Sioux City, Iowa. Heath was one of the favorites for the Labor Day classic. On his way to winning the dragster class, Heath defeated the

One of the most beautiful and fastest of the early dragsters was the *Glass Slipper,* so named because of the slipper-like silhouette of its body. Owned and driven by Ed Cortopassi, this car ran 141 miles per hour at the 1956 **NHRA** U.S. Nationals. Chevrolet presented Cortopassi with a new Chevy engine for having reached the highest speed in a Chevy-powered car.

1955 National champ, Calvin Rice, and another favorite, Bob Alsenz, who was driving a Chrysler-powered dragster. For Top Eliminator honors, Heath had to run against the Reath & Mailliard "B" Competition Coupe. Right from the start, Heath held a lead and won the race for the Top Eliminator crown. Heath's elapsed time was 10.49 seconds, and his speed was 141.50 miles per hour. That race was the last run under NHRA sanction with nitromethane as an approved fuel.

Competitors burned nitro in NHRA competition starting in 1951 and running through the 1956 season. On April 1, 1957, several of the most popular drag strips in Southern California banned the use of exotic fuels. This followed an announcement by NHRA that gasoline would be the only acceptable fuel for competition at its annual Labor Day event. Speeds were noticeably off the pace with gas. Cars that had been running the quarter at 160 miles per hour were now struggling to hit 130. The genie had been

Melvin Heath drove this homebuilt dragster to Top Eliminator honors at the 1956 NHRA Nationals, held in Kansas City, Missouri. Earlier that year, Heath, a watermelon farmer from Oklahoma, had won two NHRA regional meets. This was the last car to win an NHRA title prior to the 1957 ban on nitromethane fuel.

Powering Melvin Heath's dragster was a Chrysler Hemi engine. On top were six Stromberg 97 carburetors bolted to a Crower U-Fab intake manifold. In the mid-1950s, Stromberg carbs were inexpensive, and a lot of people knew how to modify them for nitro-burning race cars.

Don Garlits' *Swamp Rat 1* was built in 1956 and was raced through 1960. The frame rails were from a 1930 Chevrolet, with the rest of the frame made from steel tubing. In 1959 he brought this car to the Fuel and Gas championships in Bakersfield, California. After being beaten by cars running superchargers, Garlits added a blower to this car and began a legendary career in Top Fuel.

INSET:
The engine in Garlits' *Swamp Rat 1* was a 392-ci Chrysler Hemi. Eight Stromberg carburetors were mounted on a Weiand Drag Star intake manifold.

In the late 1950s and early 1960s, Setto Postoian (on the left with light-colored pants) was as big a force in Top Fuel racing as Don Garlits. In 1957 and 1958 he won the Top Eliminator titles at the ATAA (Automobile Timing Association of America) World Series of Drag Racing. The late Postoian was also credited with giving his friend Don Garlits the name "Swamp Rat."
James Genat/Zone Five Photo

stuffed back into the bottle. But not everyone went along with the prohibition. In the Roaring Twenties, the Volstead Act did little to stop the consumption of alcoholic beverages. Similarly, the fuel ban of 1957 was not about to stop all drag strips from allowing cars to run on nitro or stop competitors from "tipping" the car.

In 1959 a car club from Bakersfield, California, held a landmark event in fuel racing—the first U.S. Fuel and Gas Championships. It was the third year of the fuel ban and those

drivers choosing to run nitro in their dragsters had reached the status of rock musicians. They were the outlaws on the strip, openly defying the NHRA edict and going faster and louder than anyone ever imagined. The Smokers Inc. car club put on the event at Famoso, a World War II airstrip turned drag strip. At that time, there were no guardrails or grandstands. Thankfully, the event was held from February 28 to March 1, when the temperatures in California's central valley were moderate. That didn't stop it from being one hell of a meet.

Chris "The Greek" Karamesines was one of the first touring pros with his *Chizzler* dragster. Karamesines made drag-racing history in 1960 when he clocked a speed of 204 miles per hour. At 20 miles per hour faster than anyone else had run in a dragster at the time, it was obviously too good to be true. But it didn't keep camshaft supplier Isky from boasting about the speed in its ads. It wouldn't be until 1964 that Don Garlits would officially break the 200-mile per hour barrier. *James Genat/Zone Five Photo*

GREAT DRAG-RACING ENGINES: Ford 427 Cammer

The Ford Single Overhead Cam 427 was the only engine that ever challenged the Chrysler Hemi's supremacy in drag racing. Its unique Hemi-style head breathed easily and the single overhead cams allowed it to rev freely. Ford's Cammer was run in Factory Experimental, Gassers, Funny Cars, and Top Fuel Dragsters. There was never a street version of this engine.

When Chrysler debuted its powerful new 426-ci Hemi engine in 1964, Ford engineers knew they had their work cut out for them. The new Hemi was grinding up the competition at NASCAR tracks and on drag strips across the nation. Ford's engineering staff quickly sharpened its pencils and got out its slide rules. Within 90 days, the Ford engineers had the problem solved.

Ford, like Chrysler, was bound by the 427-ci limit imposed by both NASCAR and NHRA. Ford's engineers knew freer breathing heads were the answer to more power. What they came up with was a Hemi-style head similar to Chrysler's with one exception—they added a single overhead camshaft to each side. Officially called the Single Overhead Cam (SOHC) 427, this engine was simply called the "Cammer" by Ford enthusiasts. Ford's design concept was simple—add a set of free breathing hemispherical heads to a proven 427-ci short block. But, the design went one step further by adding a single overhead cam to each head. It was a bold move that would position Ford as a technology leader and race winner.

The Cammer engine used the same high-riser 427 cubic-inch block (4.232 bore x 3.784 stroke) that Ford had so much success with in the previous two years. The only change was an added rear oil drain. The crank and rods were the same, except for the added weight on the crank to offset the new pistons. The Cammer's forged aluminum pistons had a raised roof, with flats milled on each side for valve clearance.

On top was added a set of unique hemispherical heads that each housed a single camshaft. For this new design, Ford's engineers drew on their experience in developing overhead cam engines to race at Indianapolis. While bulky, the Cammer's new heads were free breathing and allowed the engine to rev up to and over 8,000 rpm. The single cam on each head was driven (at half the crankshaft speed) by a single 6-foot-long chain. The gear attached to the camshaft had an adjustment feature that allowed for different cam timing settings. Atop each head were two rocker shafts with roller cam followers that actuated the valves without the use of pushrods. Eliminating the traditional valvetrain allowed the engines to reach the higher rpm range.

Early tests of a single four-barrel-equipped Cammer on a Ford Motor Company dyno produced horsepower readings of over 600. The first A/FX Mustangs equipped with the Cammer used twin Holley four-barrel carbs. Fuel dragster owners soon saw the Cammer's potential. "Sneaky" Pete Robinson, who also ran a Cammer-powered fuel dragster, was the first to win a major NHRA event with Ford power. He was responsible for the development of many specialized components for the Cammer. Fuel dragster legends Connie Kallita and Don Prudhomme both found success behind the throttle of a Cammer. Unfortunately—probably because NASCAR banned it—the Cammer never saw production. It was a drag-race-only engine that reached legendary status. The 427 Cammer was one of Ford's "Better Ideas."

Don Prudhomme bought his first dragster from Tommy Ivo. Initially, he ran a Buick engine in it. Once the drag-racing bug bit him, he installed a blown Chrysler Hemi. By the look of the smile on his face, he enjoyed the ride. *Author collection*

Everyone had his sights set on one man and his Chrysler-powered dragster—Don Garlits. For years, Garlits' dragster could be seen in print ads for camshafts, intake manifolds, and tires. Each ad claimed that because of the use of a certain component, Garlits' dragster was the fastest in the nation. Many California racers considered the elapsed times quoted in those ads were pure fiction, dreamt up to sell a product. They also thought that because this Florida racer never went head to head against anyone from the West Coast, people would go on believing he was the king of the drag strip. It was time to set the record straight.

The Smokers invited Garlits to come to the West Coast for the meet. To guarantee his appearance, they paid him $1,000. At that time, no one was paid to appear at a drag race. The best

In the early 1960s, Dave Zeuschel was one of the top engine builders in the country. He excelled in building fuel-burning Chrysler Hemis, and was teamed up with some of the greatest names in Top Fuel racing. *Kent Fuller collection*

While the identification on the side of this Garlits' dragster says *Swamp Rat III*, there were actually three different *Swamp Rat III*s: A, B, and C. This is the A version that Connie Swingle crashed in Emporia, Virginia. It was built on a 115-inch wheelbase chassis and was powered by a 392-ci Chrysler Hemi.

money tracks offered was a $100 savings bond for Top Eliminator. There was very little promotion for the race—most racers and fans found out by the network in the pits. Adding fuel to the fire was a 181-mile per hour run by West Coast racer Art Chrisman just two weeks prior to the event. This was 1 mile per hour better than Garlits' advertised best.

When Garlits arrived at the event, one of the members of the Smokers remarked how Garlits' entire rig (which consisted of his brother Ed's 1953 Buick and an open trailer) and race car weren't worth $1,000. Unlike the West Coast dragsters, which were spit-polished, Garlits' dragster was more of a garden variety race car made from old Chevy rails with very little chrome and lots of dull black paint. Even the West Coast crowd was hostile to this visitor from the Sunshine State, calling him "Don Garbage." Garlits quickly quieted his antagonists on Saturday with a 9.00-second elapsed time at a speed of 172.41. But that night, a disappointed Garlits replaced the short block in his dragster, hoping for more speed. The Sunday crowd was larger than expected, estimated to be between 25,000 and 30,000. Everyone wanted to see Garlits and, without guardrails, it was difficult to keep the large crowd back from the track. Unfortunately, the man with the black dragster had a less than spectacular day. In his first-round race against Gary Cagle, Garlits threw a rod through the side of his fresh

short block. Rumors quickly circulated that Garlits had sabotaged the rod intentionally, allowing it to break and thus freeing him from the embarrassment of being defeated by his West Coast rivals.

Art Chrisman, driving the *Chrisman Cannon Hustler*, was the eventual Top Eliminator of the event. Because of the larger-than-expected attendance, the winner's purse was increased to $500.

There were several firsts at this 1959 meet. On Saturday, Art Chrisman ran his dragster without its rear tail section. Attached to the now exposed rear structure was a large cylinder that mounted horizontally, looking like an additional fuel tank. In fact, Chrisman was testing the first drag chute. The device was the brainstorm of Jim Deist, a young man who worked for the Irvine

The Greer-Black-Prudhomme dragster was initially built by Kent Fuller for Rod Stuckey. Following Stuckey's accident, the car ended up at Fuller's shop, where Keith Black and Tom Greer saw it and purchased it. The driver they selected was Don Prudhomme, who had just won the 1962 Smokers meet.

In the early 1960s, the Greer-Black-Prudhomme dragster amassed an amazing win-loss record of 236–7. While racking up those wins, it ran elapsed times in and around the eight-second mark with speeds averaging 190 miles per hour.

The Greer-Black-Prudhomme dragster is seen here at the 1963 Fuel and Gas Championships. In eliminations, it was beat by Art Malone. *Pete Garammone*

The bodywork on the Greer-Black Prudhomme dragster was designed to be easily removed. Here, the top section that covers the driver has been detached, exposing the cramped cockpit. The driver sits with the differential solidly between his legs. There is a small shield on the back of the differential housing in the area of the ring gear. On the right is a Moon gas pedal with the top cut off to clear the bodywork. The hoop on the pedal is to allow the driver to close the throttle in case the return springs break. The clutch pedal is on the left (currently being held down here by a metal hook). The long curved lever to the right is the brake handle. On the back of the engine is an oil pressure gauge—the only instrumentation on the car.

Transportation for a low-budget Top Fuel team in the early 1960s often meant hoisting the car into the back of a pickup truck. Most competitors had the luxury of a small open trailer. *Pete Garammone*

Air Chute Company. Also seen for the first time was a small fifth wheel behind the dragster driven by Bill Crossley. It was installed to prevent wheelies. The Hashim, Hilton, and Crossley dragster would soon be among the first to use a drag chute.

The fuel gauntlet had been dropped at Famoso and the fans loved it. East versus West shoot-outs would soon be the big drawing card at drag strips across the nation. The magical allure of nitro and the speeds that this enchanted fuel could produce also caught the imagination of the fans and car owners. This race also confirmed that in the future, a Top Fuel Dragster would not be competitive without a blower. Within two weeks, Garlits added one to his dragster and promptly won a race at Kingdon, California. Then he stopped at Chandler, Arizona, on the way home to Florida, and won again.

Although the NHRA had a ban on nitromethane as a fuel, other sanctioning bodies didn't. They let competitors run anything in the tank. Those racers who wanted to go faster simply didn't compete at NHRA tracks. They weren't at a big disadvantage because, at that time, most of the tracks were not under NHRA sanction. This was especially true on the West Coast, where there was the largest concentration of Fuel Dragsters.

If ever there was a car that captured the imagination of Fuel Dragster fans, it was the Greer-Black-Prudhomme dragster. When it debuted in 1962, it won eight of the first nine events in which it was entered. By May 1963, ads for Schiefer clutches declared its win-loss record to be 236 to 7. The Greer-Black-

In the 1960s, the price per gallon of nitromethane was $4.25, and a gallon of alcohol was $.55. At that time, those prices were relatively high, compared to the cost of gasoline at $.19 per gallon. Today the price of nitromethane exceeds $30 per gallon.

Prudhomme dragster would become the most celebrated fuel-burning rail of all time.

Kent Fuller originally built the car in 1961 for Rod Stuckey. It had a 112-inch wheelbase, and the engine sat with a noticeable nose-down attitude. Stuckey successfully ran the car for two months. He claimed it was consistently 5 to 10 miles per hour faster and a half-second quicker than the competition. Unfortunately, Stuckey was badly burned following an engine explosion. He eventually died from his injuries, and the car ended up back at Fuller's chassis shop, directly behind Tony Nancy's trim shop. "The car came back here and sat in the back of my lot," says Nancy. "K.B. [engine builder Keith Black] called me one day and asked if it was here." Black and Tommy Greer came out to look at the car. Greer, owner of Greer

GREAT DRAG-RACING ENGINES: The Hemi

Chrysler's original Hemi engine was the mainstay in Top Fuel racing during the 1950s and 1960s. The hemispherical cylinder heads were some of the most efficient ever designed. In addition, the basic engine was strong enough to withstand the rigors of racing without any major modifications. When the new 426 Hemi was released in 1964, it too was soon powering dragsters.

Chrysler's history with the Hemi engine began in 1951, when the first 331-ci displacement version was introduced. The basic Hemi design was used through 1958 in several bore and stroke combinations with the largest displacing 392 ci (4.00 bore X 3.90 stroke). The 392-ci version was used in Chrysler passenger cars in 1957 and 1958. It powered the first of the big-block musclecars—the Chrysler 300C. Topped by two four-barrel carburetors, the 300C's standard Hemi engine produced 375 horsepower. An optional version, rated at 390 horsepower, included a higher lift cam and increased compression.

The key to the Hemi's design was the hemispherical combustion chamber. It offered the largest volume with the minimum surface area—something engine designers always strive to attain. The placement of the valves (180 degrees apart) allowed for a "flow through" path for the incoming fuel mixture and outgoing exhaust gases. Dead center in the Hemi's combustion chamber is the spark plug. The Hemi cylinder design also allowed for large intake and exhaust valves. In addition, the Hemi responded well to cams and additional compression. They were inexpensive (in the 1960s) and could take a beating.

Hot rodders first saw the potential of the Hemi engine in the 1950s and started snapping them up for use in dragsters and street rods. The aftermarket suppliers jumped on the bandwagon and offered cams and intake manifolds to increase power. By the early 1960s, the supercharged 392 Hemi engines running large doses of nitro were belting out 1,000-plus horsepower. In the early 1960s, if a fuel dragster didn't have a Chrysler Hemi engine, it wasn't competitive.

In 1964, Chrysler introduced a new 426-ci version of the Hemi for its Super Stock Plymouths and Dodges. In record time, the aftermarket manufacturers saw that this engine would be more popular than the original and offered fuel injectors and blower manifolds. As the drag racers figured out how to make more power, many new parts hit the aftermarket shelves, including aluminum heads and aluminum blocks.

Today, those early 392 Hemi engines are being sought by collectors and are being dropped into nostalgia hot rods and vintage drag-race cars. Their renewed popularity has sent collectors scouring junk yards for the rare beasts.

The most lasting tribute to the Hemi engine design is the fact that all of the competitors running in Top Fuel and Funny Car classes today use a Hemi-style engine. Long live the Hemi!

Machinery in Cudahy, California, had the funds to go racing in style, and he knew that Black was one of the two best engine men in town. "Greer and K.B. came up, looked at it, and liked what they saw," recalls Nancy. The only thing they asked of Fuller was to change some of the diagonals on the frame.

The driver they selected was Don Prudhomme. Prudhomme had painted Tommy Ivo's dragsters and had gone on tour with him when he raced his twin-engine dragster. He eventually bought Ivo's old single-engine dragster, which he ran in B/Dragster class. The first competitive car Prudhomme drove was the Fuller-Zeuschel fuel dragster. The first time out, they set a strip record at Fontana. Then they won the 1962 Smokers meet in Bakersfield. That meet put Don Prudhomme on the drag-racing map. "That car was very competitive," says Prudhomme. It was the first car he drove with a blown engine. "You were in the biggest class out there—you were in Top Fuel—and that was *it*." Prudhomme's outstanding performance behind the wheel caught the attention of Black and Greer. He was the driver they wanted.

"When Keith called me to ask me about driving the car, I jumped at the chance," recalls Prudhomme with a smile. "I went up to the shop in Southgate. It was big—3,000 square feet or something—a place where you actually could work on the car indoors instead of out in the parking lot. He had equipment, like lathes and mills, and it was all the best." Up until then Prudhomme, like 99 percent of all drag racers, worked on a tight budget, barely able to afford the next gallon of nitro. Now he was with a well-financed team with a top engine builder. "It was great, because Keith was just so far ahead of everybody. Driving that race car was truly my big, big break in racing."

The car that Greer and Black bought was built from 4130 alloy steel. The tubing had an outside diameter of 1.75-inches with a .064-inch wall thickness. The network of tubing making up each side rail tapered together, joining at the nose. Up front, Fuller installed a Volkswagen-style front suspension that included a front cross-member incorporating a torsion bar. Fuller fabricated the front axle from 4130 tubing and added Ford spindles. He also

Tommy Ivo parked his multiengine gas burners for the speed and excitement of Top Fuel. He's seen here checking the throttle linkage on his Chrysler Hemi engine. Ivo was not only an excellent driver, but a top-notch race car builder and engine tuner. *Tommy Ivo collection*

Tommy Ivo grew up in the movie industry. When the opportunity came along to incorporate drag racing into movies, he was there with his cars and his technical expertise. Here, he talks to actor Frankie Avalon about an upcoming scene in which Avalon would play a Top Fuel driver in *Bikini Beach*, one of the movies he made with Annette Funicello. *Tommy Ivo collection*

Starting a Top Fuel Dragster in the 1960s took the assistance of a push car, or in this case, a pickup. The push vehicle would push the car to approximately 40 miles per hour. Then the driver would let out the clutch, allowing the engine to turn over, building oil pressure. The driver would then flip on the magneto, and the car would fire.

made the front wire wheels from 18-inch Borrani aluminum rims adapted to Ford spindles. Holding the front axle in alignment was a pair of hairpin radius rods. The steering drag link ran along the left side of the car, which was connected to a Ross steering gear. Fuller fabricated the small butterfly steering wheel.

Kent Fuller was one of drag racing's greatest chassis builders. When he was 11 years old, in 1947, he built his first car, for the Soap Box Derby. In 1956 he built his first dragster chassis for his brother-in-law. His next customer was Tommy Ivo, for whom he would build several chassis. He also built cars for Tony Nancy, Chris Karamesines, Roland Leong, Danny Ongias, and many others. "Kent Fuller was a very bright 'mad scientist' type of guy," says Prudhomme. "He was an artist. The kind of guy you'd find at Venice Beach painting pictures—beautiful pictures. Fuller was ahead of his time." Everyone who knew Fuller agrees that despite his various eccentricities, he built rolling works of art.

Surrounding Fuller's immaculate chassis was an aluminum body built by Wayne Ewing, who also built aluminum bodies for Indianapolis race cars. Subtle character lines and curves accented the smooth overall shape. Among the highly identifiable features of the Greer-Black-Prudhomme dragster's body were the two small scoops on the sides of the swept-up rear section. They were designed to vent air to the parachute. Ewing designed a body that was not only beautiful but was easily field stripped, giving access to the bare chassis in a matter of minutes. Cleverly placed Dzus fasteners held the bodywork to the chassis. Initially the car was painted Matador Red and then later, a bright shade of yellow. Tony Nancy trimmed the interior in black.

The G-B-P dragster used an Olds rear end, narrowed to a width of 25-1/4 inches and bolted solidly to the frame. Originally, the car was equipped with Olds drum brakes; Airheart disc drakes were later installed. The rear-end ratio was 3.08:1

Top Fuel driver Tommy "The Watchdog" Allen's firesuit was typical of the uniforms worn in the mid- and late-1960s. The suit's material was aluminized to resist the all-too-often engine fires that would engulf the driver. Only open-face helmets were available at the time. A face mask made from the same material as the driving suit was also worn. It had two ventilators to help filter out the nitro fumes. Driving a front-engine Top Fuel Dragster was a dangerous profession. *Tom Allen collection*

and was not locked. One of the later modifications was a special magnesium third member that fit into the Olds' rear-end housing. The rear tires were 10.00x16-inch M&H Racemaster slicks mounted on 10-inch-wide American Magnesium wheels.

In the early 1960s, it was unusual to have someone build an entire engine for a race car. Because of the costs involved, most competitors did much of the work themselves, farming out to the lowest bidder what they could not do themselves. At that time, Keith Black was doing more work on drag boat motors than on race cars. (At one time, he even drove a boat.) Black's precision and attention to detail were the keys to his success in building a race engine.

The 392 block in the Greer-Black-Prudhomme car came from a 1957 Chrysler. Black bored it .040 inch, but kept the stock stroke (3.900 inches). He had the Crankshaft Company grind the crank so that rod journals were all exactly 90 degrees apart. They also made sure each rod journal had the same stroke. When the Crankshaft Company was finished, Black machined grooves in the main bearing journals that aligned with the oil feed holes in the block. He also added 1-inch-wide reinforcing straps to the main bearing caps.

Black used stock 1959 connecting rods. The rods were checked for length and to make sure that the large (crankshaft) end was perfectly round and the correct diameter. The only modification was the installation of special bronze bushings into the small end to allow the pistons to float. Forged true pistons were used with a 7:1 compression ratio. Edelbrock Equipment balanced the engine's internal components.

Black didn't do a lot of porting on the 1957 cylinder heads. His theory was that the stock heads were adequate for a competition engine. He did remove irregularities and smoothed the passages within the ports. Black felt it was more important that all the ports be of the same size and shape. The intake and exhaust valves were stock, except for hard chroming on the stems. This was done to reduce friction between the valves and guides, to eliminate valve stem wear, and to reduce the valve guide clearance. Reduced clearance held the valves in proper alignment with their seats. Both rocker arms and pushrods were stock Chrysler components, but Black used Iskenderian dual valve springs.

Black felt that oiling was critical to the longevity of the engine. He used a stock pump with Torco oil. The engine produced 60 psi when cold and 40 psi when hot. The oil pump's pickup was placed at the rear of the pan. This guaranteed that the pump would have a sufficient amount of oil during acceleration, when the oil shifted rearward. Black also installed baffles that retained the oil around the pump during deceleration, when it would normally move forward in the pan. He believed that many motors failed during deceleration due to oil starvation. Many Fuel Dragster teams would drain and change the oil after every run. Black would change it after every meet. He

Not all the best Top Fuel Dragster drivers and teams came from Florida or California. The team of Barnes and Gladstone campaigned this Logghe-chassised dragster from their home state of Michigan. Named the *Michigander*, it even toured England in the 1960s.

When Don Garlits debuted this car it was painted red. Two weeks later, it was painted Garlits' standard *Swamp Rat* black. In 1964 this was the first dragster to officially run the quarter at a speed of 200 miles per hour. It also set the British land speed record of 197 miles per hour. This was the first Garlits car to have the sleek, swept-up rear section.

didn't simply pull the plug, he dropped the pan and checked for any foreign matter.

Black also modified the GMC 671 blower. On top sat a four-port Hilborn injector. The blower ran at 1.23 times crankshaft speed and was driven by a 3-inch-wide timing belt. The fuel, reportedly a 60 percent blend, came from a 3-gallon Moon tank via braided steel lines. Black ran two different blowers, depending on strip conditions.

Another major component of the success of the G-B-P car was the clutch setup. Inside the Donovan steel bellhousing was a dual disc Schiefer clutch. The pressure plate was a

In 1965, Connie Kalitta took his Ford Cammer-powered Top Fuel Dragster to the Fuel and Gas Championships in Bakersfield, California. There, he qualified fourth (7.65 seconds at 206.42 miles per hour) in a field of 65 competitors.

The *Magicar*, built by Kent Fuller, qualified 53rd at the 1965 Fuel and Gas Championships. With Jeep Hampshire driving, it had an elapsed time of 8.03 seconds and a speed of 197.36 miles per hour. This was the first dragster built with a unique rear frame-within-a-frame design supporting the rear axle. The sleek bodywork is typical of mid-1960s dragsters.

semicentrifugal type. Schiefer worked with Black on several different clutch spring combinations and friction materials. "Paul Schiefer was doing the clutch work on that car," recalls Tony Nancy. "That was the first 'slipper' clutch." When Nancy asked why the Greer-Black-Prudhomme car ran so well, Schiefer replied to him, "You gotta have a little clutch action." Looking back on the runs that Prudhomme made in the car, there was never any smoke in front of the rear tire—it was always from the center of the tire going back. The car was always

Winner of the historic 1965 March meet was Don Garlits in his *Wynn's Jammer*. This marathon meet lasted two days and had 65 Top Fuel competitors. Prior to running at the Fuel and Gas Championships, Garlits took this car to the 1965 Winternationals, where it set a speed record of 206.88 miles per hour. *Bill Pitts*

moving out of the smoke and not sitting in it. "Most of the guys would boil the tires," says Prudhomme. "They would pop the clutch and just blow the tires off." This was the commonly accepted practice of the day in Top Fuel Dragsters. When Prudhomme drove for Zeuschel, that's exactly what he did. "I used to pop the clutch on the starting line and the smoke would go forward to the engine and stay there. You'd be driving through the quarter-mile, and you'd think you were going 400 miles per hour." When Prudhomme got into

the Greer-Black-Prudhomme car, things were different. "The tires would spin, but not very fast—it would just accelerate. It was just amazing! In those days, few people knew that you needed to slip the clutch."

Running a Fuel Dragster (or any dragster) in the 1960s was much different than it is today. There were no large crews of mechanics to work on the car. There were no semitruck and trailer transporters for the cars. There were no motor homes for the drivers to relax in between rounds.

There were no areas for catered lunches for the sponsors. And most of all, there were no multimillion-dollar budgets with which to field a car. Most dragsters were taken to the track on an open single-axle trailer. Those with a tiny budget simply placed the dragster in the bed of a pickup truck. The minimum crew consisted of two people, the driver and one other person to drive the push car. Frequently, others came along to help. If not, helpers (often called "donkeys" for the level of work they were asked to do) could always be found in the pits, willing to work their butts off for a free hot dog, a Coke, and the thrill of helping a race team. Most of these guys were nitro junkies, too broke to field a car of their own, who couldn't get enough of the smell of the nitro exhaust fumes. Some of these guys were like rock groupies, following a particular car to each track, ready to do anything to get close to the action. In the 1960s, a small crew was all that was necessary, because the engines were not torn down between rounds. At most, spark plugs and oil were changed.

The starting procedure for dragsters was also different, and almost ritualistic in nature. Dragsters have never been required to have an onboard starter. The cars were started with the aid of a push car. From the staging lanes behind the starting line, the pair of dragsters would be pushed by their respective push cars three-quarters of the way down the track. There, the push cars would circle around and face the starting line. Crew members (this is where the donkeys came in) would jump out and pull the dragsters around so they were also facing the starting line. A dragster's limited turning radius meant that the cars needed to be jockeyed several times to get perfect alignment in each respective lane. With the helpers back in their push vehicles, the push car would ease up to the dragster's push bar and make contact. The push bar was designed to extend beyond any bodywork and the parachute. The drivers of both push cars would glance at each other and nod when ready to go. With the push car in contact with the push bar, the dragster driver would push in the clutch and hold up his hand to signal that he was ready. The push car would accelerate to at least 30 miles per hour. "If Keith [Black] was driving the truck, he'd honk the horn when he wanted you to let the clutch out," says Don Prudhomme. "You let the clutch out and it's really cool, because you start turning the engine over to get the oil pressure up. You'd push down on the gas and let up on it to prime all the injectors. Then you'd reach in front of you and hit the mag switch—POW—that s.o.b. would start up. I'd put a little pres-

Pete Robinson, in a dragster very similar to this one, lost his life. A degreed engineer, Robinson was one of the most astute car builders in drag racing. He invented the starter that mounted on the blower, as well as many of the high-performance components for the Ford Cammer engine.

sure on the throttle to barely crack it and it would just pull right away from the truck. Boy, that was an exciting thing!"

With the push start, there was only one chance to start the car. If it didn't fire, the competitor forfeited the round. Back at the starting line, the drivers had to circle the cars around to get into their respective lanes and face back down the track. Again, because of the limited turning radius, the donkeys were called in to pull and push the cars into proper alignment. As the car neared the starting line, the donkeys would start wiping the slicks. The car's tuner might check the engine, usually feeling the heads to see if they were up to operating temperature or to make a final adjustment to the injector. "Keith was such a clever guy," says Prudhomme. "When we started the car it was lean, so it didn't burn up a lot of fuel and it would build heat up quickly. Right before I staged, he'd richen it up. That used to piss everybody off, wanting to know what he was doing. He got quite a reputation—they'd think he was blessing the engine." Once the car was staged, it was up to the driver.

The win-loss record that Prudhomme set while driving the Greer-Black-Prudhomme dragster was amazing and established

In 1968, Larry Dixon drove the Howard Cams *Rattler* to a Top Eliminator win at the 1968 *Hot Rod* magazine meet. His best time at that meet was 6.74 seconds at a speed of 224 miles per hour. The outstanding paint on this car, as well as that of many other top West Coast dragsters, was done by George Cerny.

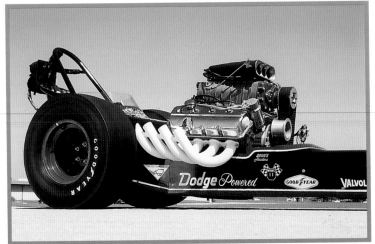

Don Garlits' Wynns Charger (a.k.a. *Swamp Rat 12C*) was beautifully trimmed in a red-and-black paint scheme. It had a 200-inch wheelbase and a 426 Dodge Hemi engine increased to 500 ci. The car was sponsored by Dodge, Wynns, and the Smothers Brothers comedy team. Garlits built the chassis and Tom Hanna built the body. Its best elapsed time was 6.87 seconds at a speed of 240 miles per hour.

the car as an icon of the front engine dragster era. Starting at Pomona on June 17, 1962, where he won the Top Fuel class, through May 5, 1963, Prudhomme established himself as king of the Top Fuel Dragsters. The cars he ran against were some of the best in the nation and so were the drivers. In establishing his 236-7 win-loss record, he defeated the likes of Kenny Safford, Tommy Ivo, Jeep Hampshire, Tom McEwen, Don Garlits, and Mike Snively. Unfortunately for them, the most feared trio in drag racing missed one of the biggest prizes when Art Malone defeated them at the 1963 Fuel and Gas Championships.

In 1963, the NHRA dropped its nitro ban, and the dragster owners flocked to the fuel ranks. Winner of the first NHRA race to be run with fuel since 1956 was Don Garlits at the 1963 Winternationals. There was no place on earth that fostered Top Fuel Dragster racing like the sunny West Coast in the early 1960s. And the best Top Fuel event each year was the annual Smokers meet in Bakersfield. It was the World Series of Top Fuel racing. Arguably, the best of those meets happened in 1965, where a field of 64 Top Fuel Dragsters were qualified for the Seventh Annual Fuel and Gas Championships.

The big show was scheduled for March 4, 5, 6, and 7. It was going to be four days of hand-to-hand combat on the Famoso drag strip. The unofficial count had 125 AA/Fuel Dragsters in the pits, ready to qualify for one of the 64 slots. On the first day, however, none of the hot dragsters were allowed to run, because of dangerously high winds. Those strong winds carried the nitro fumes out into the nearby orange groves, as the teams fired up and tuned in the pits, hoping for a better forecast for Friday. At 7:30 A.M. on Friday, the first of the Top Fuel Dragsters rolled up to the starting line.

The format for qualifying in 1965 was different from past years. Previously, anyone who showed up was allowed to race. But with so many cars in attendance, the field had to be whittled down to a manageable size. The 64 cars with the lowest elapsed times would be allowed to race on Saturday. The winner of Saturday's eliminations would sit out Sunday's eliminations, when the top 32 qualifiers returned to do battle. Sunday's winner would meet Saturday's winner for the final run on Sunday evening. Everyone wanted to win on Saturday, allowing them time to prepare a fresh "banzai" engine for the one final winner-take-all race on Sunday. The fans would see six rounds of Top Fuel on Saturday and as many on Sunday. What a weekend!

The lengthly list of Top Fuel entrants formed a Who's Who of future Top Fuel Hall of Famers. From the West Coast there was "TV" Tommy Ivo, Tom "The Mongoose" McEwen, Don "The Snake" Prudhomme, Danny Ongias, and Mike Sorokin of "the Surfers." From Florida came Don "Big Daddy" Garlits, along with Marvin Schwartz in an identical Garlits car. Michigander Connie Kallita brought his Cammer-powered dragster along with Logghe and Rupp and their hot *Slot Racer.* The rush to get into the top 32 led to some quick times by the racers. The first of the fast qualifiers was Garlits, running a swift 7.63 seconds at 205 miles per hour. Ongias then ran 7.60 seconds. Finally, Bobby Vodnick grabbed the Number One spot with a 7.32-second run. The top 32 cars all ran 7.94 seconds or quicker, and the slowest car in the field ran 8.16 seconds.

The epic event started at 10 A.M. on Saturday, when Connie Kallita, Number Four qualifier, pulled up against the Number 36 qualifier, "Gentleman" Joe Schubeck. By the end of the day, there were a lot of broken engines and 63 losers. Don Garlits outlasted them all. Saturday's win gave Garlits the freedom to sit on the sidelines and watch as the 32 fastest cars raced for the opportunity to meet him in the final. Those 32 spent Saturday night preparing for Sunday's finals.

The 33,000 fans in attendance at Sunday's finals were in for another day of outstanding Top Fuel racing. The weather had played havoc with the track, as the previous night's rain was slow in drying, delaying eliminations. Sunday's Top Fuel field was formidable. Marv Schwartz, driving a Garlits-owned car, led the way. Garlits desperately wanted to win this event. In the Sunday semifinal he took Schwartz's seat for the race against Mike Snively. Garlits was quicker off the starting line and beat Sniveley to the finish line with a 7.72 elapsed time to 7.78 for Snively. The final would be Don Garlits versus a Marv Schwartz-driven Garlits car. In 8.10 seconds the drama was over. Don Garlits crossed the finish line—winner of the 1965 Fuel and Gas Championship.

In 1966 the Fuel and Gas championships also fielded a 64-car field of Top Fuelers. It was a great show with the Surfers' Mike Sorokin coming out on top. But the drag-racing landscape was about to change. The field for the 1967 Fuel and Gas Championships shrunk to 32 cars. Funny Car racing had taken over as the hottest ticket in town, and many of the best dragster drivers defected to the new class. Don Prudhomme and Tom McEwen led the way. "I was a real dyed-in-the-wool dragster guy," says Prudhomme. "What happened was, McEwen and I started to spend a lot of time together and do a lot of match racing. He also had a Funny Car that he ran every

Tony Nancy was an early experimenter with a rear engine dragster named *The Wedge*. It almost cost Nancy his life on a run in Ohio, when the rear suspension failed, causing it to flip. *Tony Nancy collection*

chassis builders on the West Coast. These two gentlemen stretched the wheelbases on the cars they designed, and others followed. In addition to the longer wheelbases, some owners tried different aerodynamic devices. Garlits pioneered the use of a wing on a Fuel Dragster at the 1963 Winternationals when he mounted one high over the engine. Previously, a few of the Fuel Dragsters had run a small wing on top of the front axle.

Some of the experimentation with aerodynamics failed miserably. One of drag racing's biggest losses was that of Pete Robinson. Robinson, an engineering graduate from Georgia Tech, had been successful in the Gas Dragster ranks and was a late bloomer in Top Fuel. In 1966 he started running the Ford Cammer engine in a Top Fuel Dragster. Robinson was also fascinated by ground effects and the extra traction it could give him. In 1971, Robinson appeared at Lions Drag Strip with a strange looking rubber spoiler under his dragster. He claimed it was worth two-tenths of a second. To back up his claim, he was low qualifier, at 6.50 seconds. Three weeks later, at the 1971 NHRA Winternationals, Robinson was killed when his car, with the unique spoiler, veered right after clearing the lights, hit the guardrail, and disintegrated. Robinson, 37, had survived two other crashes, but this one took his life. He would also be one of the last to die in a front-engine dragster.

Another innovation in dragsters was the rear engine car. Tony Nancy, with his Wedge car in the mid-1960s, was one of the first to experiment with a rear engine dragster. Because of what was being done in England with rear engine race cars, Nancy was convinced by others that his Wedge should have a rear suspension. "We put in a suspension, but we didn't put what they had," says Nancy. "We used a torsion bar and friction shocks—not too good." The first race for the car was in the early spring in Sandusky, Ohio, on opening day at a new track. "I looked down the drag strip and walked the left side," recalls Nancy. He figured it was all new and in pretty good shape, so he decided not to walk the right side. Over the winter, the right side of the strip had sunk slightly. Nancy's first pass would be his last that day. "I left the starting line, and when 600 feet out, I felt a little sag to the car." When the car sagged, the suspension went beyond the travel of the friction shock and it locked. This put the car's rear suspension at an angle. "I was really in heavy and I felt something, but I thought I was gonna get through it. The next thing I know, it tore the right front wheel off, stuck the front of the body in the asphalt, and catapulted twice in the air. It hit the ground, way at the far end of the drag

so often in match races." McEwen struck a deal with Mattel toys to promote their Hot Wheels model cars. Mattel had researched the sport and found that Funny Cars were extremely popular. According to the deal, they wanted to run two cars, so he brought in his friend Prudhomme to run the second car. "I really didn't even like Funny Cars going into the deal, because they weren't as fast as a dragster and they had automatic transmissions. When they'd blow up, the automatic transmission fluid would pour out—it was just a mess. But we certainly needed the money—that's how it started."

Funny Cars brought a new esthetic to the drag strip, but Top Fuel still occupied the top rung in the sport because they were still the fastest. Race car builders let their minds and imaginations wander in search of new speed advantages. By the late 1960s, Don Long and Woody Gilmore were the two top strip." The car was clocked through the lights at close to 200 miles per hour. "When it landed, I was upside down. I hit my belt and fell out of the car." Nancy was badly bruised, but otherwise unhurt. His Wedge dragster was destroyed. His accident convinced others that rear engine dragsters were dangerous and discouraged them from experimenting with the design.

But an event on March 8, 1970, would be the catalyst for change. While sitting in his dragster on the starting line at Lions Drag Strip, Don Garlits was the victim of a terrible transmission explosion. The force was so devastating that it cut his dragster in two. Garlits lost part of his right foot in the explosion. "We were at Lions Drag Strip and it happened right in front of us," exclaimed Prudhomme. "McEwen and I went by the hospital in Long Beach after the race was over—we didn't want to stop during the race to go see him, of course—but after the race. And there he was with his big old wrapped-up foot and all. I thought well, at least we're done with this son of a bitch—he's outta here—we won't have to race him again. I thought for sure he'd quit, cause he was really old then, 30 or 35. Months went by and we hear that he's out building a rear engine car. All the rear engine cars we'd seen up till then were a joke."

While lying in his hospital bed, Garlits decided that he would never sit behind an engine in a race car again. All of the previous cars had high-speed directional stability problems. Back in Florida, Garlits asked his old friend Connie Swingle to help him with the construction of his new rear engine car. Garlits claims Swingle was the best chassis welder and fabricator in the business. In addition, he was also an experienced driver. Garlits credits Swingle for finding the secret to making the rear engine car work. Swingle slowed down the steering ratio. This took the sensitivity out of the steering and allowed the car to handle properly at high speeds.

When the *Swamp Rat XIV* was completed, Garlits immediately headed West. Prior to the 1971 Winternationals, there were two small events in which he would race the new car. The first event was on a Sunday at Lions Drag Strip in Long Beach. It was 5:30 in the afternoon when he pulled into the right lane. As Yogi Berra would have said, it was deja vu all over again. "It was Sunday, and I'm in the same lane, everything's exactly the same as the year before when I blew my foot off. Just for a moment, when that light was changing, I had that deja vu of that accident and of course he [Gary Cochran, the competitor in the left lane] just ran off and left me. A week later the same thing happened and Garlits lost the race again to Cochran. "By the

Following an accident in which the conventional front-engine dragster he was driving was cut in half at the starting line, Don Garlits decided to build a rear-engine dragster. He brought the new *Swamp Rat XIV* west to compete at the NHRA Winternationals. He won that event and forever changed the face of drag racing. *Don Garlits collection*

time I got to the Winternationals at Pomona," says Garlits, "which is the big race that I really went out there for, I was settled down in the car. I'd gotten all that accident of the previous year out of my system, and I went on to win the event. I'll never forget, when I pulled in there, one of the wives of one of the Top Fuel guys saw the car come in at the gate. She said, 'I hope this thing doesn't work, cause it's the ugliest dragster I have ever seen.' Well, little did that lady know that was what they were going to be looking at for a long time."

Don Garlits won the 1971 Winternationals in his new rear engine car. Not only did it win the race, it revolutionized drag racing's premier class. Within two years, all of the top drivers had switched to rear engine cars. "It was unbelievable," says Don Prudhomme. "I would say that of everything I've seen in drag racing, as long as I've been in it, that was drag racing's single biggest moment. And when he put a wing on it—we just kissed him [Garlits] good-bye—it was over with."

Twin Engine Dragsters

The early drag racers were an inventive lot and they did everything they could to go faster. They started with stripping off unneeded parts and adding speed equipment to the engine. But eventually it had to happen—the addition of a second engine. Two engines simply had to be better than one. In drag racing's relatively short history, there were some memorable twins and some that are better left forgotten.

The first twin-engine car of record was built in 1951 Joaquin Arnett of San Diego's Bean Bandits Club. It had two carburated flatheads that were mounted inline in a Model A frame. In the rear was a small Model T roadster body. Each of the two engines had a different displacement. It was initially designed to run in six classes—three dragster classes and three sedan classes, all depending on the cubic-inch displacement of the engine or engines powering the car. For the sedan classes, it was fitted with a removable full-fendered Model A sedan body that had been welded together. Arnett's plan was to run it with both flatheads connected together as a twin. He could then disconnect the link between the front engine and the rear engine and run it only on the rear engine. Finally, he could swap the front engine for the rear engine and run the car only on that engine. Thus, he could create three different total displacement combinations for three different classes.

Some early twin-engine combinations looked dangerous by today's standards. One of those oddball twins, which ran in 1957, was Johnny Sabiston's *Cannonball Express*. Sabiston had been running a rear engine flathead-powered dragster based on a 1932 Ford frame. With this configuration, he had been moderately successful, turning the quarter at speeds in excess of 113 miles per hour. Sabiston converted his dragster to a twin by hanging a small-block Chevy off the rear of the car. Both engines drove into a modified 1948 Ford rear end.

Tommy Ivo's beautiful dragster was one of the most famous twin-engine cars to ever run. Ivo worked very hard to make sure his cars were mechanically perfect and aesthetically pleasing. Ivo's twin was the first gas-burning dragster to run the quarter in under nine seconds. Twin-engine dragsters were the racer's solution to NHRA's fuel ban.

One of the first twin-engine dragsters was built by Joaquin Arnett of the Bean Bandits. It featured two flathead Ford engines (of different displacements) mounted in tandem. With the addition of the Model A sedan body, the car could be run in the coupe class. *Don Cox*

Changing from dragster to coupe class was as easy as dropping on a Model A sedan body. The body's panels and fenders were welded together and all the glass was removed, including the windshield. This particular car allowed Arnett to run in six different classes, depending on the engine combination and whether or not the sedan body was fitted to the chassis. *Don Cox*

The first successful twin-engine car was the *Bustle Bomb*, owned and driven by Lloyd Scott. Up front was an Oldsmobile engine and in the rear was a Cadillac engine. The Cadillac engine hung so far over the rear, it looked like a turn-of-the-century lady wearing a bustle. Both engines drove through the same rear end. Scott's outlandish-looking dragster was the first to go 150 miles per hour. Prior to the *Bustle Bomb*, most twins were flathead-powered and didn't have sufficient torque to pull the extra weight of the second engine.

The 1957 NHRA fuel ban made competitors look at twin-engine configurations more seriously. Gasoline limited the amount of power that could be produced by one engine. One solution to the dilemma was to add a second engine. In the late 1950s, there were few rules restricting the design of multi-engine dragsters. Two V-8 engines could be successfully installed in a dragster by one of three basic ways. The engines could be mounted side-by-side, either in a vertical orientation or canted outboard at the top as viewed from the front, or the engines could be mounted in line. Each design had its own benefits and inherent flaws. The greatest burden confronting drivers running a twin was the extra weight of the second engine. This was substantial, even with a small-block Chevy, the lightest V-8 available. The twins also needed stronger frame rails and larger front tires, adding even more weight. Doubling the power never equated to doubling the speed.

From 1958 through 1963, twin-engine cars were at their peak. One of the first successful twin-engine dragsters was the *Howard Cam Special*, first driven by Glen Ward. It was built by Howard Johansen, founder of Howards Cams. In 1961, Jack Chrisman drove it to Top Eliminator at the NHRA's U.S. Nationals. It featured twin blown Chevys mounted side by side. Under the unusual twin-engine dragster column was the *Iron Mistress*, built by Bill Coburn. It had a small Messerschmidt body and featured twin blown Chrysler Hemis. It had two rear axles and two pairs of slicks. Coburn and Neil Leffler took turns driving this ungainly looking dragster. In 1958, Mickey Thompson built a four-wheel-drive twin-engine dragster. It featured two injected Chrysler Hemis mounted inline; one engine drove the front wheels, and the other engine drove the rear. This car would eventually serve as the prototype for Thompson's land-speed attempt *Challenger*, which was powered by four Pontiac engines. In 1960, James Warren drove a twin-engine dragster sponsored by Bob's Muffler Shop. It was an inline configuration with a carburated small-block Chevy in front and a blown Chrysler Hemi in the back. Its top speed was 169 miles per hour.

Tech inspector at Paradise Mesa drag strip, Jim Nelson (kneeling in foreground) is carefully examining the front engine as other members of the Bean Bandits club look on. In dragster form, the car ran with a cut-down Model T roadster body. On the rear was a set of old tires turned into slicks by virtue of the fact that the tread had worn off. *Don Cox*

Tommy Ivo was a West Coast youngster who had been racing a Nailhead Buick-powered dragster in the gas class. To go faster, his options were to install a blower on his current dragster or build a twin. He tried the blower, but found that it reduced the reliability of the Buick engine. So, like so many others, Ivo hopped on the twin-engine bandwagon. While most of the other racers were running the small lightweight Chevrolet engines, Ivo would continue to use the reliable Buick engine for his twin.

Kent Fuller had built the chassis for Ivo's single engine car and Ivo returned to Fuller for the twin. In 1959, Fuller's chassis design looked similar to a Chassis Research frame with a short wheelbase and triangular-shaped rollbar. The frame Fuller built was similar to the single engine car Ivo had, except it was a little beefier and a little wider to accommodate the two engines. "I drove Fuller crazy with that car," says Tommy Ivo. "We took the exhaust and leaned it back at the same angle as the rollbar,

so everything looked right aesthetically." There wasn't enough room for the eight exhaust pipes in between the two engines, so two of the stacks were routed down beneath the car.

The chassis had a wheelbase of 92 inches, a front tread width of 57 inches, and a rear tread width of 38.5 inches. The frame was designed to use the engines as structural elements. In the late 1950s, there were two choices for frame materials: mild steel and chrome moly. Fuller preferred chrome moly tubing. Chrome moly was half the weight of mild steel, but just as strong. The two main lower frame members had a diameter of 2 inches and the upper support rails were 1.75 inches in diameter. The rollbar was also made from 1.75-inch tubing.

The small aluminum body on Ivo's twin was built by Michael Scott, a local tin man who had built bodies for other dragsters and for Indianapolis race cars. The body wasn't simply a sheet of aluminum wrapped over the frame rails; it had several interesting character lines that added style to the shape. In the back, a Deist drag chute was faired into the body. Below it was a chrome push bar cut in the shape of a wind-up key for a child's toy. Chrome was also added to the front axle, hairpin radius rods, and the steering gear. The frame was painted black and the body was orange. A young painter from the San Fernando Valley by the name of Don Prudhomme painted Ivo's car.

Ivo's approach to the twin configuration was to install the engines side by side, with both blocks angled slightly outboard. This allowed the use of a narrower frame. This engine configuration also allowed him to mate the two engines' ring gears so a single clutch could be used. But this arrangement also created a series of engineering challenges that Ivo would have to face, such as how to reverse the direction of rotation of one of the engines and how to balance the chassis so that the car would not be prone to wheelstanding.

Ivo selected two 1957 Buick blocks with an original displacement of 364 ci (one of the engines was pirated from his single-engine dragster). Each was cylinder-bored 3/16 inch to 4-5/16 and a 0.60 stroke was added to the crankshafts by C-T Automotive. This increased the displacement to 467 for each engine, resulting in a total of 934 ci. Ivo selected Jahns pistons and had them fitted to the stock connecting rods. He used 1960 Buick cylinder heads on each engine. The ports were enlarged and polished and the combustion chambers were polished. Isky dual valve springs were used on the stock valves.

The problem of reversing the second engine's direction of rotation was solved by camshaft grinder Ed Iskenderian.

He ground a camshaft for the right-side engine, which allowed it to run in the opposite direction. The distributor drive gear was cut in reverse so that the distributor and subsequent oil pump drive would turn in the standard direction. This allowed conventional off-the-shelf oil pumps and distributors to be used. Timing for both cams was identical. Matching Vertex magnetos and Hilborn fuel injectors were installed. A single fuel pump was installed on the left-hand engine, which fed both sets of injectors. The pump was a large Hilborn unit designed for a blown engine. Ivo installed 18-inch long pipes on each cylinder. He had run 36-inch pipes on his single-engine dragster, but found that the shorter pipes worked better on the twin. The only other modification to the engines was to rework the oil pans to accommodate the angled installation of the engines.

The mating of the engine's ring gears was a good idea for connecting the engines, but it had some initial "teething" problems. Each engine was equipped with a Scheifer aluminum flywheel with two ring gears installed. Traditionally, the ring gear on a flywheel is retained by the interference fit between the gear

Squeezing two Buick V-8s into a dragster chassis took some doing. The close proximity of the engines allows the gears on the flywheels to mesh. To mesh flywheel gears, one of the engines had to turn in the opposite direction. This was accomplished with a specially ground camshaft. Because of the limited space between engines, two of the exhaust stacks are routed downward.

As driver Tommy Ivo stands by his car following a run, chassis builder Kent Fuller gathers up the drag chute. With the addition of a second engine, twin-engine dragsters were approximately 600 pounds heavier than their single-engine counterparts. Stopping power became an important factor in the design. *Kent Fuller Collection*

A youthful-looking Tommy Ivo holds up his hand to signal the driver of the Cadillac push car, future drag-racing legend Don Prudhomme. Prudhomme toured with Ivo, helping him with the car. He also painted this car. Ivo sold Prudhomme his old single-engine dragster and, as they say, the rest is history. *Tommy Ivo collection*

The two Buick engines in Ivo's dragster drove into a single rear end. The engine on the left rotated in the standard direction and was equipped with a dual-disk clutch. Ivo sat with his legs to the right of the quick change differential.

and flywheel. Ivo needed to ensure that the ring gears would be able to transmit the necessary torque without slipping off of the flywheel. To accomplish this, he welded six equally spaced tabs to each ring gear so each could be securely bolted to its respective flywheel. One of the problems Ivo encountered when meshing the ring gears was an interference when heat built up in the clutch. When several runs were made in quick succession, the heat generated by the clutch made the flywheel and ring gears expand. This caused the teeth on one flywheel to bottom-out on the other flywheel, exerting excessive side loads on the rear of the crankshafts. This in turn caused damage to the rear main bearings. Ivo's solution was to carefully monitor the amount of heat in the clutch. In addition, he had the crankshafts hard-chromed to extend their life.

Kent Fuller built the chassis for Tommy Ivo's twin-engine dragster. The design included a fore-and-aft adjustment to the engine location to help fine-tune the balance of the car. Ivo required the skid bar-type of roll cage and also wanted the exhaust stacks laid back at the same angle as the front struts of the cage.

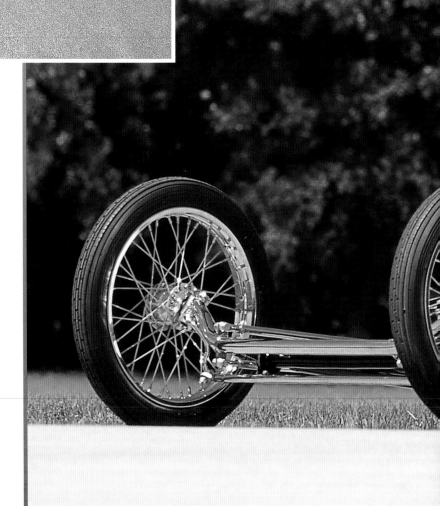

Dode Martin and Jim Nelson owned the Dragmaster chassis company. For the 1960 racing season, they built a twin-engine dragster that they named the *Two Thing*. Nestled between the strengthened frame rails were two small-block Chevy engines that had been bored and stroked to 354 ci each. Similar to Ivo's twin, the *Two Thing*'s engines were joined at the flywheels. At the 1960 U.S. Nationals, it set the fastest speed of the meet, at 171.10 miles per hour, and was awarded the trophy as the Best Engineered Car. *Pete Garamonne*

The single clutch on the left-hand engine was a Scheifer dual disc with a steel floater plate. It drove into a Cook Cyclone in-and-out box, then into a short driveshaft to the 1948 Ford rear end with a quick-change center section. Differential gearing was 2.94:1. The rear end was not locked, but was a conventional open design that Ivo felt would be safer if one of the axles broke. The brakes were from a 1952 Lincoln.

To assist in balancing the car, Ivo and Fuller designed a certain amount of flexibility into the chassis design with respect to the location of the engines. The motor mounts allowed a 6-inch adjustment, fore and aft. When Ivo made his first runs with the car, he put the engines all the way forward. From these early tests, he determined that the engines should be located 4 inches rearward. He also moved the rear axle 3-1/2 inches forward and extended the front of the frame 2 inches. This chassis balancing act gained Ivo one full second in elapsed time and several miles per hour in top speed. On Ivo's third trip to the track, he tied the elapsed time record for Gas Dragsters. He soon set and reset the record. In doing so, Ivo often match raced Fuel Dragsters and repeatedly beat them. In February of 1960, Ivo drove his twin down the quarter in 8.95 seconds to be the first Gas Dragster to run the quarter in less than nine seconds. "My twin was the hottest running car around," exclaims Ivo. "It was the first car into the eights on gas—it was a bad son of a gun."

In the late 1950s and early 1960s, Dode Martin and Jim Nelson's Dragmaster Chassis company manufactured one of the best ready-to-race dragster chassis available. They not only

built dragsters but ran one of their own chassis in competition. For the 1960 season, they tried their hand at building and running a twin. To identify it from their single engine dragster, they called the twin the *Two Thing*.

The *Two Thing*'s chassis was similar to the standard Dragmaster chassis built for a single engine, except it was widened to accept the two Chevy engines they planned to run. In the area of the engines, they added steel plates, which tied the upper and lower frame members together. Similar to Ivo's twin, *Two Thing* had its engines mounted side by side, angled out, with the flywheel gears meshing. Martin and Nelson also provided for fore and aft adjustment of the engine package to fine-tune the chassis balance. Unlike Ivo, they added crankshaft-driven blowers. The Chevy engines were bored and stroked, increasing the cubic-inch displacement from 283 to 354 on each engine. Both engines ran Racer Brown cams. The cam in the engine on the right side was ground so that engine would run in the reverse direction. Like every car the Dragmaster team of Martin and Nelson ever built, the *Two Thing* was well-engineered, ran fast, and looked good in its gold and red paint. The problem was that it weighed 1,900 pounds.

At the 1960 U.S. Nationals in Detroit, the *Two Thing* was favored to win Top Eliminator. It had turned the fastest

speed of the meet at 171.10 miles per hour. In addition, it won the Best Engineered car award, presented by *Motor Trend* magazine. The *Two Thing* also took the AA/Dragster class with a winning time of 10.10 seconds at 168.53 miles per hour. In the runoff for Top Eliminator, the *Two Thing* was eliminated in an early round by the eventual winner, Leonard Harris, in the *Albertson Olds* single-engine dragster. The *Two Thing* was not the only twin-engine dragster at the 1960 Nationals. The large group of twin-engine dragsters included Tommy Ivo, Jack Chrisman driving the *Howard Cam Special*, Detroit area racer Donnie Westerdale in *Dubble Trubble*, Jack Moss with his twin-Chevy-powered *Two Much*, and Bill Tibbles in his *Hurry Up III*. The *Two Thing* was the most successful of the group, but it still couldn't beat a good running single-engine dragster.

Eddie Hill has a long history in both drag-race cars and drag-race boats. In 1961 he ran a twin-engine dragster that used a pair of Pontiac engines. He designed and built the dragster himself, including spraying on the Popsicle Purple metal flake paint. Hill's twin-blown Pontiacs drove into a 1948 Ford rear end with two center sections. The most unusual aspect of the car was Hill's rear wheel rim design. Each rear wheel mounted two slicks. At the 1961 Nationals, Hill's twin-engine dragster created a stir when the dual slicks tore up the asphalt at the starting line.

One of the most successful twin-engine dragsters was the Nye Frank and John Peters' Quincy Automotive twin, better

GEORGE HURST

George Hurst was one of the most influential men in drag racing. He took an interest in the sport in the late 1940s, when he made a few passes down a drag strip in his passenger car. Soon, he started building motor mounts that allowed the average hot rodder to swap the then-new overhead valve engines into an early Ford chassis. Hurst was a born marketer. Prior to a West Coast trip, he shot an extensive series of how-to photos on the installation of his new motor mounts. Upon hitting the Golden State, Hurst made an appointment with Wally Parks, then the editor of Hot Rod magazine. Parks was so impressed by the mounts, the quality of the photos, and the technical notes Hurst provided that he scheduled an article for a future issue.

Hurst's next big development was his floor shift conversion kit. Manual transmission cars of the late 1950s and early 1960s were burdened with balky

George Hurst (center) was an innovator, inventor, and a big supporter of drag racing. He also knew how to get his product's name before the eyes of potential customers. Here at the 1961 U.S. Nationals, he presents Jack Chrisman (left) with two prizes—the trophy for being 1961 NHRA points champion, and the keys to a brand-new Thunderbird. *Greg Sharp collection*

column shifters. They were fine for the elderly couple on their way to the Early Bird Special, but woefully inadequate for a young Turk trying to run through the gears in a hurry. There were a few conversion kits on the market, but they lacked quality. Hurst designed a new floor shift linkage that was strong and looked good. It was so good that Pontiac Motor division offered it as a dealer-installed option on three-speed manual shift 1961 Pontiacs. Soon Hurst released its replacement four-speed shift linkage. In 1962, if a performance car didn't have Hurst linkage, it wasn't taken seriously.

The Hurst Hemi Under Glass was one of the first projects to come out of the Hurst Performance Products engineering lab. It was a 1965 Barracuda with a Hemi engine installed in the rear. It thrilled race fans with its wild wheelstanding antics. Hurst Performance Products also built the Hurst Hairy Olds. It was a 1966 442 equipped with two Olds Toronado blown 425 ci motors in a tubular frame with Toronado final drives. It was the first 4x4 all-wheel-drive exhibition car. With former Top Fuel driver "Gentleman" Joe Schubeck at the wheel, the Hurst Hairy Olds was a four-tire smoking success. In 1968 Hurst was back at it again building Hemi Darts and Hemi Baracudas for Chrysler's Super Stock effort.

Hurst's biggest contribution to mankind, other than Linda Vaughn (Miss Hurst Golden Shifter), was the Jaws of Life, a hand-held device for prying open or cutting apart cars that have been damaged in an accident. He offered an early prototype to the Los Angeles Police Department in the mid-1960s. His first version was heavy and had 100-foot-long hydraulic hoses that made it cumbersome. He continued to refine his design by cutting weight and adding an auxiliary motor. Today, Hurst's Jaws of Life are standard equipment at fire and police agencies across the country.

George Hurst was an inventive visionary and a slick promoter. His products are widely recognized for being built to the highest standards. Anyone involved in drag racing will quickly recognize the Hurst name, not only for his excellent performance products, but also for his personal contributions to the sport and society.

known as the *Freight Train*. In 1960, Frank and Peters built a twin-engine dragster with a pair of fuel-injected 330-ci small-block Chevy engines mounted inline. The chassis was home-built and heavy. As with most race cars, the final configuration of the Quincy Automotive twin evolved over several years. First, a single crank-driven supercharger was added to the front engine; then, a top-mounted supercharger was added to each engine. Eventually, the frame would be replaced in 1966, reducing the weight to 1,650 pounds.

Following its run, the *Dubble Trubble* twin Chevy dragster is pushed down the return road, while two stockers race on the track. Donnie Westerdale sits in the driver's seat with his helmet off and sunglasses on, contemplating changes to prevent another wheelstand. Due to the extra weight, most twin-engine dragsters used larger front tires. ©*James Genat/Zone Five Photo*

In 1961, John Peters met the man who would be the most auspicious driver of his twin-engine dragster—Bob Muravez (a.k.a. Floyd Lippencotte). Muravez had been successfully racing his own BB/Dragster in the Southern California area. One week prior to a match race, he broke his engine and didn't have the money to fix it. "John Peters, whom I hardly knew, walked up to me and offered me a motor to run my match race," recalls Muravez. Muravez was stunned, but he accepted Peters' offer. He pulled the engine out of Peters' twin, installed it in his dragster, and promptly won the match race. When Muravez returned the engine, Peters asked him what his future was without an engine for his dragster. "I said, 'I don't know, I don't have a lot of money,'" says Muravez. "Then he offered me a ride in the twin-engine car." It was the opportunity of a lifetime for Muravez. Upon joining the team, the gregarious Muravez had a hard time getting close to Nye Frank. Unbeknownst to Muravez, Frank had recently lost two good friends in drag-racing accidents, and he didn't want to get too close to Muravez in case he also got hurt.

Detroit area racer Donnie Westerdale drove the *Dubble Trubble* twin-engine dragster, seen here at Detroit Dragway in a mid-track pushbar-dragging wheelstand. Wheelstands occur when the tires get too much bite and the torque of the engine causes the pinion gear to climb the ring gear. One unique aspect of this dragster is the unusual rollbar-mounted parachute. ©*James Genat/Zone Five Photo*

For three months, Muravez drove the car every weekend at Lions and San Fernando drag strips in what could be considered a driver's training course. Peters and Frank wanted him to gain experience in their unique car. One of the unusual characteristics of the car that Muravez had to master was the unique way it handled. "It was unlike any other dragster at the time," says Muravez. "The front end would move up and down 10 inches from the static state." The Quincy Automotive car was built on a short 96-inch wheelbase. (By comparison, Muravez's single-engine dragster had a wheelbase of 92 inches.) The theory of its design was to allow the front end to rise upon acceleration,

effectively transferring the extra weight of the additional engine to the rear wheels. Unfortunately, the car's steering geometry caused the car to move to one side of the track upon acceleration, and to the other side upon deceleration. Muravez recalls, "At the start, as the front end moved up, the car would move right. And as you shut the car off at the end, the front end banged down and the car would move left. So you had to turn the wheel a quarter of a turn as you throttled in and out." Muravez claims that as long as his timing between throttle and steering was correct, it was an easy car to drive. "I was very young and very impressionable and I thought I had the dream of a lifetime driving that car." Getting off the starting line cleanly was also a problem, because the lightweight Chevy engines didn't have an abundance of torque. It wasn't unusual to see a twin-engine car like the Quincy Automotive twin bog 50 feet off the starting line. It took a keen sense of clutch timing and throttle input to accelerate smoothly—a skill Muravez soon mastered.

John Peters and Nye Frank teamed up to build a twin-engine dragster that was initially sponsored by Quincy Automotive. Their dragster featured two small-block Chevy engines mounted in tandem. When this photo was taken, it featured a single crankshaft-driven supercharger. *Bob Muravez collection*

The Peters and Frank *Freight Train* twin-engine dragster had a considerable amount of travel to the front suspension. Upon acceleration, the front end would lift approximately 5 inches. Because of the steering gear geometry, it would steer to the right as the front end rose. It took a good driver to be able to feed in the proper amount of throttle to keep the engine from bogging and a steady hand on the steering to keep the car going straight. *Bob Muravez collection*

Peters and Frank continued to refine their engine combination and made more power. Unfortunately, the extra power also meant more broken parts. "I was making a pass at the Beach [Lions Drag Strip in Long Beach, California] when just before the lights, the motors went up to the moon—something broke in the drivetrain," recalls Muravez. "I always looked out the left side, and I noticed that up front a piece of the body was peeled open, as if you had taken a big can opener and opened it up from the inside out." Muravez shut the car down and was able to get it safely stopped. When he got out of the car he had a little trouble walking. "All of a sudden, I noticed I wasn't walking very straight. The clutch had come out by my left foot and took the heel off my shoe." Following the clean removal of Muravez's heel, the clutch continued through the cowling. "It didn't bother

my foot, but it was amazing that I was so close to that type of thing and didn't get hurt."

The Peters and Frank Quincy Automotive twin with Bob Muravez at the wheel soon became famous by clocking the first 180-mile per hour speed in the quarter. The first big race it competed in was the 1962 Bakersfield Fuel and Gas Championships. "In those days you didn't really qualify; every Double A Gas Dragster was pre-entered," recalls Muravez. The race officials simply paired off the competitors and they raced until there was a winner. Muravez's first race was against a young guy from

This later photo of the *Freight Train*, driven by Bob Muravez, was taken after the frame was stretched. After clearing the traps with chute in full blossom, Muravez is looking over his shoulder to find the car he just raced. *Bob Muravez collection*

What do you do when you've just won the 1963 Winternationals and you don't want anyone to know that you're the driver? You allow one of the crew (Rex Slinker) to accept the trophy from the Queen. Hiding behind Slinker is the winning driver, Bob Muravez, a.k.a. Floyd Lippencotte. Sitting on the hood of the Pontiac push car is Nye Frank, who seems to be amused by the situation. On his right is co-owner Frank Peters. *Bob Muravez collection*

DRAG-RACING MUSEUMS

Most automotive museums don't pay homage to drag racers. Museums dedicated to other forms of auto racing may mention drag racing only in passing. It wasn't until Don Garlits opened his Drag Racing Museum in 1984 that the sport's history was given a permanent home. In 1998 the NHRA opened its museum in Pomona, California. Like Garlits' museum, the NHRA museum focuses on drag racing, but also includes land speed racers, some dirt-track cars, and a few choice hot rods and customs.

Garlits is a national treasure in the eyes of all drag racers. "Big Daddy," as he is known, has done it all. He first ran down a drag strip in 1952. He perfected the rear engine dragster and set numerous records. Within the first few minutes of the year 2000, he was running down the quarter-mile in a Top Fuel Dragster competing against another legend, Shirley Muldowney. In 1976, Garlits realized that this young sport had no archive of cars or memorabilia and no place to honor its pioneers. He started to collect cars that had been run by other racers and to restore some of his own old race cars. In 1984 he opened the original 25,000-square-foot facility in Ocala, Florida. Today, this extensive collection of race cars fills 50,000 square feet. If you happen to visit his museum, keep your eyes open for the man himself. Big Daddy is an active participant in the museum's day-to-day operations, and you might just run into him.

In 1992 the NHRA opened a modest Historical Services Department, under the watchful eye of the late John Zenda. Initially, Zenda's job was to organize the inaugural NHRA California Hot Rod Reunion. The success of that first reunion fostered the idea for an NHRA museum. Zenda's Historical Services office was in a small industrial complex across the street from the Pomona Drag Strip. As

Don Garlits' Museum of Drag Racing is filled with some of the most historic and significant drag-racing cars of all time. In addition to a large collection of Garlits' own Swamp Rats, there are dragsters that were driven by Pete Robinson, Chris Karamasines, Tommy Ivo, and Don Prudhomme. In addition to dragsters, there is at least one example of every type of race car ever driven down a strip.

In addition to drag-racing cars of all types, the NHRA Museum has on display a few Indy cars, Bonneville record setters, dry lakes racers, hot rods, and custom cars. Within the cases that line the wall are drag-racing artifacts and memorabilia.

The NHRA Motorsports Museum
1101 W. McKinley Avenue
Pomona, California
(909) 622-2133
nhra.com

Don Garlits' Museum of Drag Racing
13700 S.W. 16th Ave.
Ocala, Florida 34473
(352) 245-8661
garlits.com

word spread, the collection of old race cars and memorabilia increased, overwhelming the space. After Zenda's passing in 1993, hot rod historian Greg Sharp was hired to continue the work, which included finding a permanent home for a museum.

In 1997 the NHRA started renovation of a 29,000-square-foot building on the Pomona Fairplex grounds. In 1998 the new museum was complete and was officially opened to the public on April 4. More than 60 cars are exhibited, along with display cases of racing memorabilia. Many special events are held at the museum throughout the year, including twilight cruises during the summer months. The museum's staff members have also continued to spearhead the annual NHRA California Hot Rod Reunion, held each year in Bakersfield, California. There, they keep the historical flame burning, honoring those who have contributed to the sport.

These facilities provide an excellent window on drag racing history and are worth a pilgrimage for devoted fans. Many of the cars in this volume are on permanent display at one of these museums and were photographed with their staffs' cooperation and assistance.

In the late 1960s, Shirley Muldowney drove a twin-engine dragster built by her husband, Jack. It featured twin blown small-block Chevys mounted in a Don Long chassis. Muldowney eventually moved on to fuel Funny Cars and then Top Fuel Dragsters. *Shirley Muldowney collection*

the Midwest named Connie Kallita. "We were in the staging lanes getting ready to race and Kallita walked over to me and said, 'Where do you want me to put your name on my car?' " Muravez was confused, but Kallita went on to explain. "I'm the Bounty Hunter, and as I beat people, I put their names on the car and I just wanted to know where you want your name." Muravez noticed there were little asterisks after some of the names. "Well," Kallita continued, "everytime I beat you again, I put an asterisk by your name, so I can keep count." Muravez thought for a second and replied, "Tell you what, Mr. Kallita, why don't you put my name on the bottom of your car so that when you crash trying to beat me, everyone will know the reason why." Muravez proceeded to blow Kallita's doors off, as well as everyone else's, on his way to winning the 1962 Bakersfield meet.

Muravez's joy of winning one of the biggest drag-racing events of the year was soon dampened by an ultimatum from his father, who owned a successful business. "He gave me three options," says Muravez. "I could stay in racing and work in the family business, but I would never own a piece of it. Or I could continue to drive and go work somewhere else. The third option was for me to quit racing altogether and, in time, take over the family business." In June 1962, Bob Muravez retired from racing. The sudden retirement of such a rising star was covered by both major drag-racing publications, *Drag News* and *National Dragster*. Muravez's father relented and allowed him to go to the races to crew, but it was understood that he would not drive. The first replacement driver for the Peters and Frank dragster

was Craig Breedlove. He had difficulty with the way the car moved around on the strip. Breedlove was also building a car (with the help of Peters and Frank) in which he would attempt the land speed record. To focus on his land speed attempt, Breedlove asked to be relieved of the driving responsibilities. Tom McEwen was next in the seat and he also had problems with the way the car handled. Mickey Thompson gave it a try, but he couldn't make it go either. Bill Alexander was the next driver to get behind the wheel. Alexander worked at it for three months, but the car was not responding with him behind the wheel. The world's quickest and fastest dragster had not made a competitive run for five months.

Muravez did his best to tutor each new driver, and Peters and Frank made mechanical changes to suit each driver's personality and needs. One night in December 1962, while at Lions Drag Strip, Muravez was talking to driver Bill Alexander about the handling of the car. Alexander turned to him and said, "You don't know what you're talking about, Bob. They've made so many changes to this car that even you couldn't make it go straight!" Muravez replied, "Well, let's try." Muravez put on the driver's gear, while Alexander hid in the push car. The instruction Muravez received from Peters and Frank was to make an easy pass, because Alexander might be right. Muravez pulled up to the line and winged the throttle three times. "I felt like I was home again," says Muravez. "It had been almost six months since I'd been in the car. I just let the clutch out, nice and easy, and the car just roared off the starting line and went straight." Muravez made a clean pass, shut it off, and pulled the parachute. Once the car slowed down, Muravez pulled the car off to the side, got out, and lit up a cigarette. "I could hear a tremendous amount of cheering and screaming from the fans," recalls Muravez. Peters and Frank pulled up in the push car and were noticeably upset, but they didn't say anything. Then Bill Alexander got out of the car and had a terrible look on his face. Muravez asked what was wrong. "John looked at me and said, 'We told you to make a nice easy pass.' I said, 'I did! The car went straight as an arrow, it was a nice clean pass, and I shut if off in the first light.'" Peters went on to explain to Muravez that he had just set a new speed record of 185 miles per hour and came close to the elapsed time record. Muravez's one-word reply was, "Wow!"

Because of Muravez's promise to his father not to drive a race car, he couldn't ride in the car as it was being pushed back to the pits. Mickey Thompson, owner of Lions Drag Strip, knew how to fire up a crowd, and he did his best following

After the NHRA lifted its ban against nitromethane, a few of the twin-engine dragsters switched from gas to nitro. The Frye Brothers twin-injected Buick exhibits the trend to longer wheelbase dragsters that came about in the late 1960s. This photo also shows the simplicity of the 1960s-era rigs that carried competition cars to the track. ©*Larry Davis*

Because of the extraordinary weight of Ivo's four-engine dragster, it took the largest drag chute ever installed on a dragster to slow it down. Here, the chute has just blossomed and has pulled the rear wheels off of the ground. Ivo hated the car because it was so heavy. And with no suspension, it rode extremely rough. *Tommy Ivo collection*

Muravez's record-setting run. Sitting in the car, an uneasy Alexander accepted the accolades from the crowd. Following that event, there was talk of cutting up the car and doing something else. Muravez was also torn between his intense desire to drive and his promise to his father. Drag racers have often been compared to drug addicts. There is a high that comes from sitting in the seat of a race car and having it perform well. Muravez was hooked. He decided to drive again, but would use the name of the car owner, John Peters. Only a few people were in on the secret. He would suit up out of the sight of the crowd and get out of the car at the far end of the track and someone else would sit in the car when it was pushed back to the pits. This elaborate charade allowed him to race while concealing his true identity from the fans and his father.

The next big race for the Peters and Frank twin-engine dragster was the 1963 NHRA Winternationals. With Muravez behind the wheel, the big dragster was back in its usual high speed form. "There were so many Double A Gas Dragsters in the field that we made seven passes that day, which is unheard of today," says Muravez. The four low elapsed-time cars came back to run off for Top Gas Eliminator. With darkness setting in, Muravez once again lined up against Connie Kallita. "I raced him again and beat him worse the second time," cackled Muravez. "That was the ninth time I'd raced him since the Bakersfield meet in 1962, and beat him every time." Every time they raced, Muravez made a point of looking under Kallita's car for his name and then he would ask, "Connie, why haven't you put my name on your car yet?"

As 1963 drew to a close, the Peters and Frank twin-engine dragster was listed as Number One in the *Drag News* Top Ten Eliminator list for Gas Dragsters. "Sneaky" Pete Robinson wanted to have the Number One spot so he'd get more money while on tour in 1964. Robinson challenged the Peters and Frank twin, and the race was set to run at the San Gabriel drag strip in California. At the time, Top Gas Dragsters were getting $100 to $200 to appear at a match race. For this race, the Peters and Frank car was guaranteed $1,000. Pete Robinson, who was one of the top racers of the day, wasn't guaranteed a dime. Mel Reck was the track announcer and Steve Gibbs had just come onboard to help in the tower. Gibbs was also a part-time journalist who wrote about the Southern California drag-racing scene. As the cars were coming to the starting line, Reck shut the mike off and said to Gibbs, "We gotta give this guy his own identity," referring to Muravez's clandestine driving of the powerful twin-engine dragster. Gibbs said, "Call him Irving Lippencotte III." Something got lost in the translation because when Reck turned the mike back on, he referred to Muravez as "Floyd Lippencotte Junior." In addition to getting an alias under which he could race, Muravez also beat Robinson and retained his Number One spot on the *Drag News* list.

The Peters and Frank twin dragster soon became known as the *Freight Train*. But not because of the locomotive-like sound from the twin engines. The name was coined at Fontana, a track at a higher altitude than most of the Southern California drag strips. Fontana also had three distinct bumps at the end of the quarter-mile. Because of the high altitude, the cars running on gas had a tendency to detonate when they went through the lights. "When I went over the three bumps at the top end," says Muravez, "the car would load and unload, load and unload, putting out three big puffs of black smoke." Judy Thompson, former wife of Mickey Thompson, told him that the car looked like a "freight train" chugging up a grade. The name stuck.

The *Freight Train* was parked in 1971 when the NHRA dropped the Gas Dragster class in December of that year. The American Hot Rod Association (AHRA) had already dropped the class at the end of the previous year. Fuel Dragsters and Funny Cars were now the rage. Prior to its retirement, the *Freight Train* was fitted with a pair of blown Chrysler engines and the wheelbase was stretched to 210 inches. This combination produced a 6.9-second elapsed time and a speed of 211 miles per hour, making it the fastest and quickest Gas Dragster ever. "We were mad that they dropped the class," exclaims Muravez. "Point blank mad—how dare they do that." But as Muravez looks back on it now, closing the books on twin-engine dragsters was the right thing to do.

In 1960, Tommy Ivo figured that if two engines were good—four must be better. Ivo started with four Buick 401-ci engines. He had C-T Automotive build stroker cranks for each of those engines that would increase the displacement to 454 ci. Each engine was built identically with Jahns pistons, Isky cams, Hilborn fuel injectors, and a modified Vertex magneto. The four engines totaled 1,816 ci with an estimated horsepower of 1,720 (430 per engine). The two engines on the right side of the car drove the rear wheels, and the two on the left drove the front wheels. Unlike Ivo's twin, these engines were not joined at the flywheel to the adjacent engine. The tandem pairs were joined at the crankshaft by a double roller chain on specially designed sprockets. At the back of the right pair of engines was a double-disc Schiefer flywheel and clutch that drove into a Ford truck rear end. The left bank of engines drove forward into a Halibrand Championship rear end. The front wheels were fabricated from Buick rims with steel disc centers and the rear wheels were

Halibrand magnesium. Both front and rear were shod with slicks. The steering gear was from a 1953 Mercury. And like his twin, there wasn't room for all 16 exhaust pipes between engines. Only 14 were routed up, with two exiting under the car.

Kent Fuller built the frame for Ivo's four-engine creation. During the one-year construction of the car, Fuller and Ivo constantly butted heads. "Fuller was sick of it," recalls Ivo. "He didn't like the idea of four engines." Fuller's contention was that a single engine dragster with a blower was faster. "He fought me for a year over the thing," says Ivo. "We could have had it done in a couple of months, but he'd build other cars, stopping work on my car. That didn't set very well with me."

The chassis that Fuller built for Ivo's four-engine car was constructed with 3-inch-diameter chrome moly tubing. The rollbar in the rear was similar in design to Ivo's twin dragster. The seat, trimmed in leather by Tony Nancy, was positioned in the center of the car. When Ivo sat in the car, his legs were positioned slightly to the left and over the rear axle. The seating position was skewed because of the large center section on the rear axle. To Ivo's right was the brake handle. The small aluminum body was built by Bob Sorrell and painted by Don

Wild got wilder when Tommy Ivo parked his twin-engine dragster in favor of a four-engine monster. Construction started in 1960 and took one year to complete. The chassis was built by Kent Fuller. Each of the four Buick engines displaced 401 ci. The pair on the right drove the rear wheels and the pair on the left drove the front wheels. From the starting line, this car could smoke all four tires the length of the strip. *Tommy Ivo collection*

Prudhomme. Named *Showboat*, Ivo's four-engine dragster was an amazing car to watch in action.

Just as Ivo finished the four-engine car, NHRA came to him and said, " We trust your equipment, and you can continue to run your own car. But in the future, we're going limit it to two motors. Because if that car runs well, we're going to have a dozen four-motor cars out there." They went on to explain that the four-engine cars were too heavy and if they got out of control, the risk was too great that they might careen into the stands. "Well, that broke my heart," says Ivo. "But I had the corner on the market with that being the one and only—and that's why that car got to be my signature car."

Without a class to run in, Ivo's four-engine *Showboat* went on exhibition tour and even appeared in a 1960s surf movie, *Bikini Beach*, with Frankie Avalon and Annette Funicello. "I hated that car, because it was a terrible car to drive," says Ivo.

"It was like driving a 200-mile per hour Sherman tank." With four iron motors and no suspension, the ride was exceptionally rough. "If you hit a bump at the other end, it bounced like a rubber ball," says Ivo. In addition, the 4,000-pound weight of the car made Ivo a little leery of driving it. He was afraid that if the chute didn't come out, the car would "end up in the next county." Soon after the four-engine car was completed, fuel was once again legal for use in NHRA competition, and Ivo became a member of the fuel fraternity.

Multi-engine cars were a major part of the development of drag racing in the 1950s and 1960s. Each was an engineering marvel. In theory, they all should have been world beaters, but there was no way to get the power of extra engines without their added weight. Although their time came and went, each multiengine car showed an amazing amount of seat-of-the-pants engineering and inventiveness.

3-1
ct

Super Stock to Pro Stock

Not all cars that raced down the quarter-mile were specially built hot rods or dragsters. Virtually everyone got their first ride down the quarter in a car that ran in a stock class. For the average racer, running a car in a stock class at the drags was the easiest way to get involved; it simply meant showing up at the track, paying an entry fee, getting classified, and dropping the hammer on the family sedan. In the early days of drag racing, car ownership by young adults was not as prevalent as it is today. Many of those in line to race were driving their parents' cars. One young man was a regular drag strip participant with his mom's new 1959 Pontiac four-door sedan. It had a V-8 with a three-speed column shift. That tricky column shift linkage was never intended for racing and he blew several transmissions—all of which he claimed were defective parts. On one return visit to the dealership for transmission warranty work, his mother was asked by the service writer if she had ever raced her sedan, to which she indignantly answered no. The service writer then asked why she had exhaust cutouts on her car. Needless to say, her son never raced his mom's car again.

Until the advent of the overhead valve engine, factory stock cars were not thought of as something that would be raced on a drag strip. They were either the engine donor for a hot rod or race car, a tow vehicle, or everyday transportation. In the early 1950s, the cars with the most powerful engines, Chryslers and Cadillacs, were expensive and too heavy to be made into race cars. The early 1950s Oldsmobile was the first factory stock car to be seen regularly on a drag strip. While not cheap, an Olds was more reasonably priced than a Chrysler or Cadillac, had a terrific Hydra-matic transmission, and was a little lighter than a big Caddy. A well-tuned 1950 Olds with a V-8 could run the quarter in just under 18 seconds at a speed of 75 miles per hour.

1963 shaped up to be an epic year in the struggle for Super Stock supremacy. Pontiac's entry that year was the Catalina sport coupe with the 420-horsepower 421-ci engine. Every effort was made to make the car lighter, including use of aluminum body components and drilling the frame.

ABOVE:

In the early 1950s, the new Olds overhead V-8 was one of the hottest engines around. It also meant that the Olds was one of the quickest passenger cars. Here at Santa Ana drag strip, a 1950 four-door model powered by a 135-horsepower engine in the near lane takes on a mildly customized 1953 Olds. *Greg Sharp collection*

INSET ABOVE:

Not everyone could afford a race car in the 1950s, so the only alternative was to race the family sedan. Because of the convenience of nearby drag strips, as compared to the dry lakes, it was an easy way to get into drag racing. *Don Cox*

ABOVE, RIGHT:

The interior of a 1961 Super Stock was identified by the Hurst floorshift conversion, oil pressure and water temperature gauges under the instrument panel, and a Sun tachometer mounted on top of the instrument panel. Seat belts were not required for competition in 1961. *James Genat/Zone Five Photo*

RIGHT:

In 1961, Ford upgraded its 390-ci engine to 401 horsepower, with the addition of three two-barrel carburetors. Unfortunately, Ford didn't offer a four-speed transmission or locking rear axle as its competitors did. This 1961 Starliner has a slight nose-high attitude, typical of the early 1960s Super Stock cars. On the rear is a set of Atlas Bucrons, soft butyl rubber tires that were the poor man's cheater slicks. *James Genat/Zone Five Photo*

By the mid-1950s, the greatest number of drag strip entries were in the stock class. This was due in part to the burgeoning popularity of drag racing and the fact that every major car manufacturer had an overhead valve engine. One car in particular was instantly popular—the 1955 Chevy, with its new 265-ci V-8. Now drag-racing enthusiasts didn't have to fork over the family fortune for an Olds 98. A new Chevy One-Fifty two-door sedan with a V-8 had a manufacturer's suggested price of $1,627. For an additional $55, the Power Pack option could be added, which included a four-barrel carburetor. For an additional $100, an overdrive could be specified, which included a standard 4.11 rear end. For less than $1,800, anyone could have a lightweight six-passenger family car that would run excellent times at the strip and be one of the hottest cars on the street.

In 1956 stock cars were classified by advertised horsepower-to-weight ratios (shipping weight divided by horsepower). Because of increasing horsepower ratings from the factory, the calculations

for class designations were adjusted annually. In 1956 there were four classes for stock cars: A, B, C, and D. Cars running in A stock were restricted to those from 15 to 16.99 pounds per horsepower. Cars falling into A Stock in 1956 were Power Pack Chevys and all four-barrel equipped Pontiacs and other cars with large displacement engines. B stock cars were those having 17.00 to 20.99 pounds of weight per horsepower. Most of the V-8-powered cars in this class had a two-barrel carburetor. Because of their lighter weight, six-cylinder cars like the Hudson and Nash ran in B stock. C stock (21.00 to 26.99 pounds per horsepower) comprised lighter-weight six-cylinder cars and heavy-weight V-8s. D stock class comprised the heaviest cars with the smallest engines. Cars that ran in D stock in 1956 were six-cylinder Chevy station wagons, six-cylinder Ford Crown Victorias, and all DeSoto and Dodge sixes.

The rules for stock cars in 1956 were minimal. The engine had to be the same type, year, and model as the car in which it was run. The car had to be as it was built on the assembly line,

In 1961, Chevrolet released its new 409 engine. "Dyno" Don Nicholson won Stock Eliminator at the NHRA Winternationals in his 409-powered Impala. For the U.S. Nationals later that year, he ran in a class designated as O/SS (Optional Super Stock). This class was designed for Super Stocks with the latest factory-built, over-the-counter modifications. Nicholson's Impala ran the same heads and dual quad intake that were released for production on the 1962 409 engines. ©1996, NHRA Photographic

In 1962 the NHRA Winternationals and U.S. Nationals Super Stock titles were both won by 409-powered Chevys. The 409 engine was distinguished by its scalloped valve covers and aluminum dual quad intake manifold. Rated at 409 horsepower, it could easily rev to 6,000 rpm. Performance options for the Chevy that year included a four-speed transmission and positraction rear end.

with no aftermarket equipment installed. A maximum of .060 cylinder overbore was permitted, but no other engine modifications were allowed. Headers and dual exhaust systems were permitted, but exhaust cut-outs were not. Devices that prevented the rear springs from winding up on acceleration were considered a safety factor and were permitted under the rules. Stock car contestants could run tires that were one size larger or one size smaller than originally specified for the car by the manufacturer. Any gear ratio listed by the manufacturer as being optional was also allowed. Many of the cars in the 1950s were customized and a certain amount of customizing was allowed in the stock classes.

In 1956 there were some factory cars that exceeded the horsepower-to-weight restrictions of A stock; these cars were placed into Gas classes. Considered "factory hot rods," a Chevy with the dual quad option was moved into C Gas, along with the DeSoto Adventurer. B Gas cars in 1956 included the Chrysler 300-B, a Ford with the Interceptor engine, a Mercury with the M-260 engine option, a Plymouth Fury, and a Pontiac with the 287 horsepower engine. Seat belts were not required in any of the stock classes. They were required in the Gas classes only if the body had been modified.

In 1957 the heat was turned up on the horsepower race bringing it up to full sizzle. At the same time, the AMA

Don Nicholson drove this sleek 1962 Chevrolet Bel Air to his second consecutive NHRA Winternationals Mr. Stock Eliminator win. The Bel Air was the favored body style, because of its fastback roofline and light weight. ©1996, NHRA Photographic

In 1962, Dave Strickler drove this 409-powered Chevrolet Bel Air sport coupe in the Super Stock class. In 1963 he campaigned it in the A/Stock class. It was sponsored by the Ammon R. Smith Chevrolet dealership in York, Pennsylvania. A close inspection of the front bumper reveals two brackets that were tow bar attachments, so the car could be flat towed to each race track. *Author collection*

The Super Stock wars were going great guns in 1962, especially on the East Coast. Freedom "7" Dragway in Virginia Beach, Virginia, offered $250 in cash to the Top Stock Eliminator, but only $100 to the Dragster Top Eliminator.

(Automobile Manufacturers Association) wanted to cool the horsepower competition among manufacturers. They proposed a voluntary ban on the direct support of racing by all automobile manufacturers. In theory, the manufacturers agreed to the AMA's ban, but they all continued to design and build higher-horsepower cars and to support racing, even if it was through the back door. Multiple carburation was the underhood rage in 1957, with dual quads and tri-power setups leading the way. Chevrolet added fuel injection to the mix and Ford offered a McCullogh supercharger. In Detroit, a fresh generation of engineers was making its mark on new car designs. This new breed understood hot cams and multiple carburation. Engine

engineer Dick Keinath was a new employee at Chevrolet. Days after he took delivery of his first new V-8-powered Chevy, he was standing in his driveway in ankle-deep snow installing a hotter cam. In a few short years, Keinath would be involved in development of the 409, and eventually he became the father of the big-block Chevy engine.

Under the guise of "police specials," the factories kept churning out higher cubic-inch-displacement engines as the 1950s came to a close. The General Motors cars (Chevrolet and Pontiac) had the edge over the competition, because of the optional four-speed transmission that could be specified behind several optional V-8s. It was also at this time that the competitors in the Stock classes, who were not allowed to use racing slicks, found alternative tires that gave them better bite than the factory rubber. Atlas Bucrons and Vogue tires were two of the early favorites. Open exhausts were now allowed in stock classes, and the more serious competitors fitted tubular headers to their cars. A 1959 Pontiac Catalina, sponsored by Royal Pontiac, would be the first stock car to exceed 100 miles per hour and run in the 13-second bracket on a drag strip (13.91 second elapsed time at 102 miles per hour). A few years earlier, Pontiacs were the preferred vehicles of elderly widows and spinster librarians. Now they were setting records on the drag strip and on NASCAR tracks. For the upcoming decade, manufacturers began working on a new image—performance.

At the 1959 U.S. Nationals held at Detroit Dragway, many of the people in the stands and wandering through the pits were executives and engineers from the Big Three's nearby engineering centers. This was precisely the exposure that Wally Parks wanted for drag racing. "In 1959, we were working very hard to gain the attention of the Detroit industry," recalls Parks. "At the 1959 Nationals we had Tex Colbert, who was the president of Chrysler, and Ed Cole, who was the president of Chevrolet, standing there making bets on whose model would win."

The group at Pontiac, headed by Bunkie Knudsen, accomplished the most in the least amount of time. For 1960, Pontiac introduced new big port heads, 11:1 forged pistons, streamlined exhaust manifolds, and a new cam. This combination produced 363 horsepower with tri-power carburation. A Borg Warner T-10 four-speed transmission was optional, along with a limited-slip rear end offered with a large selection of gear ratios. In 1960, Pontiac also introduced a stylish set of wheels that included finned aluminum brake drums. Jim Wangers, driving a 1960 Pontiac Catalina sponsored by Royal Pontiac, took Super

Chevrolet produced over one million passenger cars in 1962. Their popularity was enhanced by the performance and celebrated image of the 409 engine. Here, two 409-powered Impalas square off. The car on the left has the rear of the hood raised up. This was done to allow more airflow through the engine compartment. The car on the right has added a homemade hood scoop. *Author collection*

In 1960, Jim Wangers drove a Pontiac Catalina, sponsored by Royal Pontiac, to the Stock Eliminator win at the U.S. Nationals. Wangers continued to drive Royal-sponsored cars and in 1962 raced this 421-powered Catalina sedan. The 1962 Pontiacs were very competitive on the strip, but because of their higher cost, they were not as popular as the Chevys, Fords, or Mopars. *Jim Wangers collection*

The favored body style for serious Super Stock competitors was the lightest one available, which was usually the two-door sedan. The rear wheels on this 1963 Dodge are painted half-and-half, black and white. This was a common practice in 1963, in order to help detect rear tire spin.

Stock honors at the 1960 U.S. Nationals. His closest competition was Pete Seaton in a comparably equipped 1960 Catalina. Wangers' fastest time at the event was 13.81 seconds at 104 miles per hour. Royal also sponsored another Catalina that ran in the Super Stock Automatic class. It ran the same 363-horsepower engine, but was backed by a four-speed Hydra-matic transmission. It ran the quarter-mile in 14.5 seconds at 98 miles per hour. In the final for Super Stock Automatic, the Catalina was beaten by Al Eckstrand's 1960 Plymouth.

The wake-up call for Chevrolet, Ford, and Chrysler was earsplitting. A Pontiac, known as the favorite of senior citizens, was now the Super Stock performance king. How embarrassing! In 1961, Chevrolet introduced its new 409, and Ford increased the displacement of its FE engine from 352 to 390 ci. But, it would be the 409 that would reign supreme in 1961.

Only two 409s were in competition at the NHRA's 1961 Winternationals in Pomona. At that time, the 409 engines were not available through regular dealer channels, nor were they available off the showroom floor. The 409 was legal for NHRA because Chevrolet had provided the Automobile Manufacturers

Association (AMA) with specs for the engine. It was an unusual back-door deal that brought the 409 to the races that year.

In the early 1960s, Bill Thomas had Chevrolet factory connections and prepped Corvette road race cars. He regularly used a local tuner, Don Nicholson, who worked for Service Chevrolet running the chassis dynamometer. Nicholson was also a whiz with Corvette fuel injection systems. Thomas was aware that Nicholson had been cleaning up on the local drag strips with his 348-powered 1960 Biscayne. Through Vince

Piggins, Chevrolet's high-performance rep, Thomas arranged for Nicholson to get one of the first 409 engines for the upcoming 1961 Winternationals.

To get ready for the season, Nicholson purchased a new, white 1961 Impala two-door hardtop with a 348-ci engine, four-speed transmission, and Posi-Traction rear axle. Upon delivery, he took the car to his friend Jerry Jardine, who

would build him a set of headers in anticipation of the soon-to-arrive 409. The 348 and 409 had the same external dimensions, making Jardine's task easy. Just days before the race, the new 409 engine was delivered. Nicholson tore it down and carefully reassembled the new engine. On the Wednesday prior to the Friday opening of the 1961 Winternationals, Nicholson was lowering the new engine into his

Impala. Thursday was spent with final installation details, and that evening Nicholson got some much needed sleep. Before going to bed, he gave the keys to a friend and asked him to drive the car around the city all night to break everything in. Nicholson wanted all the gears and wheel bearings seated before the race. It's unknown how many street races the docile-looking Impala won that night.

The only other 409-powered Chevy at Pomona in 1961 was a red Biscayne owned by Frank Sanders from Phoenix, Arizona. His car was also set up by Nicholson. Super Stock Class eliminations were held on Saturday. The final run came down to Sanders versus Nicholson with Sanders taking the class win. On Sunday's final run for Stock Eliminator, the pairing was the same, but the outcome was reversed, with Nicholson taking the honors. Nicholson ran the quarter-mile consistently in the mid- and low-13-second range at speeds as high as 108 miles per hour.

Ford fans were somewhat disappointed that their hot 390 engine wasn't more competitive. Just prior to the Winternationals, Ford released an aluminum tri-power intake manifold that mounted three Holley two-barrel carburetors. That setup bumped the horsepower of the 390-ci engine from 385 to 401. Unfortunately, Ford did not have an optional four-speed transmission or locking rear axle. Pontiac revised its camshaft design for 1961, gaining only five horsepower and losing its Super

The parade of stockers at the 1963 Winternationals was impressive, as two long lines of factory sedans rump-rumped down the strip with open headers. A few years earlier, the presence of stock cars was just filler for the dragsters, competition roadsters, and coupes—now they were one of the main events. *Greg Sharp collection*

Leading the charge for the Dodge Super Stocks in 1963 were the candy-striped sedans of the Ramchargers. The Ramchargers was a club made up of Chrysler engineers. The club's first drag-racing effort was a gasser. It was a natural move to Super Stock when Chrysler started to produce cars for the class. The circular "T" sticker on the windshield was a designation for those cars eligible for a trophy run. *Dave Crane collection*

Stock crown in the process. The engineers at Chrysler were not competitive, nor were they asleep. They were the first to introduce ram-induction, and their constant work on that concept would soon reap some big rewards.

In 1961 the U.S. Nationals were moved to their permanent home—Indianapolis. Rule makers had to contend with a gaggle of parts being released by the factory on an almost daily basis. General Motors was the worst offender, with a long list of new over-the-counter parts for both Chevy and Pontiac. Chevy produced new heads, a new cam, and a new dual quad intake for the 409. Pontiac increased the displacement of its 389 engine to 421 ci, and added a new cam and dual quads. Factory cars with over-the-counter parts were designated to run in the Optional Super Stock (OSS) class.

Quarter-mile times were now in the mid-12-second range with speeds up to 110 miles per hour.

The Super Stock wars cranked up to a fever pitch in 1962. Ford released its 406-ci engine rated at 405 horsepower, with three Holley two-barrel carburetors, backed by a new four-speed transmission. Chevrolet returned with the 409 rated at

409 horsepower with dual-quads. Pontiac's beefy dual quad Super Duty 421 was rated at 405 horsepower. The Pontiac was also the most expensive Super Stock in 1962, with the 421 engine option alone listing for an additional $1,334.24.

Dodge and Plymouth were now full-fledged members of the 1962 Super Stock fraternity with their new 413 Max Wedge engines. Available rated at either 410 or 420 horsepower, depending on compression ratio (11:1 or 13.5:1), these engines cranked out 460 ft-lb of torque. Both engines were fitted with a unique cross-ram intake with dual Carter AFB carbs. Swoopy cast-iron exhaust manifolds connected to 3-inch exhaust pipes with built-in cut outs. Only two transmissions were available with the Max Wedge engines: a Borg Warner-built heavy-duty three-speed manual with a Hurst shifter, and the TorqueFlite. Automatic transmissions were always seen as the last thing you wanted in a performance car, but Chrysler's TorqueFlite changed everyone's perspective. Dodge and Plymouth offered something the other Super Stock competitors couldn't match—a lightweight body and low cost. The average Dodge or Plymouth B-body was 200 to 300 pounds lighter than a Chevy, Ford, or Pontiac. These cars were also the easiest on the pocketbook, with the 410-horsepower engine option listing for a mere $374.40. The Dodge and Plymouth cars offered more performance for the dollar than any other car in 1962. Unfortunately, they were the ugliest cars on the market.

The official kickoff of the 1962 drag racing season was the NHRA Winternationals. In the past, stock cars had always been the filler between the "real" races with real race cars—Dragsters, Coupes, and Altereds. In 1962 the factory-built cars took on a new status at the strip, drawing as much attention as the purpose-built race cars. Because of the increasing horsepower-to-weight ratios, the NHRA opened a new class at the top of the stock category called Super Super/Stock. Designated as SS/S for manual shift cars and SS/SA for automatics, these classes gave the fans an on-track comparison of what Detroit had to offer. Towing all the way from the East Coast was Dave Strickler with his white 1962 409-horsepower Bel Air. From Northern California came the team from Bill Walter's Ford. Foothill Motors from nearby Fontana wheeled in with its new Dodge Super Super Stock. Previously, cars running in the stock classes were privateers with little or no sponsorship. Now most of the Super Super Stock competitors and a few of the cars in the lower stock classes had the sides of their vehicles embla-zoned with a new car dealership's name in permanent paint. Spectators saw cars on the strip that they could identify with. And the paint schemes let the fans know where these high-performance stock cars could be bought.

The new 406 Fords and Max Wedge Mopars made an impressive showing at the Winternationals. But for the second straight year, the GM cars were dominant in Super Super/Stock. Hayden Proffitt, driving a 421-powered Catalina, took class honors, running the quarter in 12.75 seconds at 111.94 miles per hour. The final for Stock Eliminator saw "Dyno" Don Nicholson running against Dave Strickler. Both drove white Chevrolet Bel Air sport coupes with 409 engines and both were sponsored by Chevrolet dealers. When the starter raised the flag, Nicholson's holeshot gave him a lead he never relinquished. Even though Strickler ran a quicker time (12.55 to 12.84 seconds), he followed Nicholson for the length of the strip. For Nicholson's efforts, he was presented with a color television and a trophy. He also had bragging rights for the year, which opened the door for match races across the country. In September, the U.S. Nationals were held in Indianapolis. Hayden Proffitt, now driving a 409-powered Bel Air, took the Stock Eliminator title.

The technology of the day for stock class cars was rather simple compared to that of today's modern cars. In the early 1960s, all competitors subscribed to the theory that to get the best weight transfer for better traction, the front of the car had to be raised and the rear of the car lowered. This conclusion was drawn from the fact that upon acceleration, the front end raised and the rear end squatted. Why let the engine do the work of shifting the car's center of gravity, when a few shims in the springs or turns on the torsion bars could raise the front end? Chevy and Pontiac competitors replaced the rear coil springs with softer versions to let the rear of the car settle as low as possible upon acceleration. Pontiac's sturdy four-link rear suspension needed no extra attention. Dodge, Plymouth, and Ford all had parallel leaf-spring rear suspensions. The torque of the rear axle would wrap the rear springs until they snapped back into shape. This induced some nasty oscillations in the rear axle, causing uncontrolled wheel hop. To counteract this phenomenon, several small clamps were added along the length of the spring. Aftermarket traction bars were allowed under the rules, and a majority of competitors used them.

There were a few other modifications that could legally be made to the cars running in the stock classes in the early 1960s.

CORVETTES IN COMPETITION

One of the hottest stock cars in the late 1950s and early 1960s was the Chevrolet Corvette. Straight from the showroom floor, the Corvette was the closest thing to a real race car anyone could buy. The Corvette offered a light-weight body, a high-winding small-block V-8, and, in 1957, a four-speed transmission. In stock form, they were designated to run in the Production Sports classes, and if modified, they ran in the Modified Sports classes. Corvettes remained popular at the drag strip until the inexpensive Super Stock cars began to flood the streets in 1962.

In the early 1960s, two Southern California Corvettes made their mark in drag-racing history. Late in 1961, Brendan Grassman bought a used 1961 fuel-injected Corvette to replace the 1958 Corvette he had been drag racing. Even though the car had been raced quite a bit, Grassman knew that with the right equipment and tuning, it could run even quicker. He turned to Chevy engine master Don Nicholson for the tune-up. Grassman also added a set of Horsepower En-

John Mazmanian initially bought his 1961 Corvette to drive on the street and to race occasionally. As his desire for speed escalated, the look and makeup of his Corvette changed. These changes included cutting the rear wheel openings for larger slicks and adding a rollbar.

gineering headers and a Moon scattershield. After tearing up the smaller local drag strips throughout the winter of 1961, Grassman knew that to have the ultimate bragging rights in Southern California, he would have to run—and win—the upcoming 1962 Winternationals. He had Earl Wade, another Chevy wizard, rework a set of heads, and Grassman added a set of American Mags, which were legal for the B/Sports Production class. Driving the car at the Winternationals would be Hugh "Putzel" Osterman, who would go on to drive altered roadsters and dragsters. Osterman made a clean sweep of the class and went on to race for Street Eliminator, just losing to a Pontiac Tempest powered by a 421 engine. Throughout the event, Grassman's Corvette ran elapsed times in the 12.70 range, with speeds just under 110 miles per hour. Soon after the Winternationals, Grassman blew the engine in the Corvette, and it was parked. His interest turned to dragsters, and in 1968 the Corvette was sold to its current owner.

The most famous Corvette that ever ran the quarter was John Mazmanian's candy apple beauty. In 1961, Mazmanian wanted a car that was a little faster than the supercharged 1957 Ford he had been driving on the street and occasionally taking to the drags. Mazmanian wanted to step up in looks and performance, and one day went to his local Chevrolet dealer to look at the large stock of new Corvettes. Running the dealer's chassis dyno was Don Nicholson. Nicholson pointed out a red fuelie to Mazmanian that, when run on the dyno, developed more horsepower than any of the others. Mazmanian bought it and raced it occasionally. He also let his nephew, Richard Siroonian, borrow it for cruising to the local drive-in restaurants. Mazmanian soon found out that his nephew was street racing the car. He set down an ultimatum: "If you want to race, you have to do it on the strip!"

Success was only a quarter-mile away, as Mazmanian's Corvette won the C/Modified Sports class at the 1962 Winternationals, running the quarter in 12.07 seconds at a speed of 115.23 miles per hour. Mazmanian was intoxicated by the allure of speed. Soon, the Candy Apple Persimmon Corvette was sporting a 471 blower and going a lot faster. Eventually, with a 671 blower and other modifications, it ran its best elapsed time and speed of 10.90 seconds at 130 miles per hour. Mazmanian's Corvette was featured on the cover of both Hot Rod and Rod & Custom magazines in 1963. From the Corvette, Mazmanian moved on to his famous A/Gas Supercharged Willys Gasser, and eventually to Funny Cars.

Under the hood of Grassman's 1961 Corvette was a 315-horsepower fuel-injected Chevy engine that was tuned by Chevy wizard Don Nicholson. This engine, backed by a four-speed transmission and 4.56 rear axle, was a combination solid enough to run the quarter in 12.70 seconds at a speed of 110 miles per hour.

In the late 1950s and early 1960s, Corvettes were the hottest production cars available. The Corvette's light weight, high-revving small block, and superb performance options made the sports production class one of the most hotly contested. In 1962 this 1961 Corvette, owned by Brendan Grassman and driven by Hugh "Putzel" Osterman, won the B/Sports Production class at the NHRA Winternationals.

Under the hood of John Mazmanian's Candy Apple Persimmon Corvette was a blown small-block Chevy. The best quarter-mile time for this car was 10.90 seconds at a speed of 130 miles per hour.

After-market gauges could be added and everyone had a tachometer. Anyone ordering a new 409 Chevy with a four-speed was given a Sun tachometer as part of the package. Everyone else bought one at the local speed shop and mounted it high on the steering column or on top of the instrument panel, where it could be easily read during a run. Shift points were a constant topic of conversation between competitors, and the tach became the touchstone to extracting as much performance as possible. The standard factory four-speed linkage was not intended for speed shifting. The Hurst Competition Plus shift linkage was everyone's favorite replacement. Pontiac was a step ahead of the other manufacturers and offered a Hurst shifter as a factory option. Tubular headers were allowed and, like the Hurst shift linkage, all the serious competitors had them. Some competitors made their own, and a few were purchased from fledgling header manufacturers like Jardine or Stahl. Tire manufacturers were also getting on the bandwagon, and they started to build slicks especially for the stock classes. Stock class cars were limited to 7-inch rear tires. Cassler and M&H were the two brands of choice. Most serious competitors in the stock classes ordering a new car to race at the strip speced it out as a radio and heater delete. This saved a few dollars and a few pounds of weight.

While the rules were maintained at national events, they were severely bent at match races. There was a "run what ya brung" attitude among the competitors and track owners. As long as the car looked like it was basically stock, it was allowed to run. It was at these match races that entrepreneurial Super Stock owners made their money. They would often book races on Friday night, Saturday night, and Sunday afternoon, all at different tracks. They were paid strictly for appearing and for being able to run down the strip—not on whether they won or lost the match race, although each competitor wanted to win to enhance his reputation. The track owner would frequently give the racer an additional $50 if he would tow his car around the local drive-in restaurant circuit the night before the race. Super Stock match races usually paired a local favorite against an out-of-town rival. It was a simple format that still exists today. In addition to the hype surrounding the Local Hero versus the Visiting Villain, there was also the brand versus brand battle. It was easy to get the crowd worked up over which make of car was best. No track owner worth his salt would ever book cars from the same manufacturer against each other. Chevy versus Chevy or Dodge versus Plymouth did nothing to stir the passions of brand loyal fans and would have been bad for business.

The Z-11 Chevy engine was based on the 409, with a slight stroke to increase displacement to 427 ci. It also featured new heads and a high-rise intake manifold. All Z-11s were fitted with an aluminum water pump as a weight-saving feature.

Chevrolet released a limited number of Z-11 optioned Impalas for the 1963 racing season. These specially built cars had aluminum front ends and were delivered without heaters or radios. Only 57 were built before General Motors withdrew its support of racing activities.

In 1962 another class was added to the NHRA roster—Factory Experimental, designated FX. Factored by cubic-inches-to-weight, there were three classes: A/FX, B/FX, and C/FX. These new factory hot rod classes replaced the Optional Super Stock (O/SS) class. Factory Experimental offered an interesting mix of cars for the fans. The concept was to allow competitors to build cars from over-the-counter production parts. This allowed the introduction of smaller, lightweight bodies with engine and transmission packages not offered as standard options. At the 1962 Winternationals, Hayden Proffitt ran a 1962 Tempest coupe in the A/FX class. Built in Mickey Thompson's Long Beach shop, the Tempest was powered by a dual quad 421-ci Pontiac engine that drove through the Tempest's swing axle rear end. This car took the A/FX honors with a 12.37 elapsed time at a speed of 117.27 miles per hour. "Dyno" Don Nicholson took B/FX in a Chevy II station wagon, powered by a 360-horsepower, 327-ci fuel-injected Corvette engine. Nicholson's winning time was 12.55 seconds at 108.96 miles per hour.

Depending on the sanctioning body, the Z-11 Chevys ran in Super Stock, A/Factory Experimental, or A/Modified Production. As the race season progressed, the frail aluminum fenders and bumpers soon became bent and dented. The Earl Evans–sponsored Z-11 has had the two outboard headlights removed so fresh air could be ducted to the carburetors. *Author collection*

Tom Sturm took advantage of the new FX rules and built a car that would eventually win the NHRA Stock Car Points Championship in 1962. Sturm started with a 283-powered Chevrolet Bel Air sport coupe. He added every Corvette component he could buy at the Chevy dealer's parts counter, including a fuel injection camshaft, a four-speed transmission, and a Rochester fuel injection. At 11 pounds of weight per cubic inch, he was classified in C/FX. "I picked the class where the record was low, and I figured that I could break both ends of the record every time I raced," recalls Sturm. He hit the road and ran 14 weeks in a row, setting the class record at every track. "I drove the car by the tach and shut off when I got so far down the track to keep the elapsed time within breaking distance," says Sturm. "There was a lot of psychology to runnin' that year!" Sturm eventually whittled the C/FX record down to 14.15 seconds at 100.24 miles per hour. With each new record came additional points toward the NHRA Championship. Sturm's combination was durable and fast. For winning the

Stock Car Championship in 1962, Sturm was presented with a new Hurst Pontiac Gran Prix at Indy, which he promptly drove back to the West Coast while a friend towed his race car.

The year 1963 was shaping up to be a colossal one for Super Stocks. General Motors, Ford, and Chrysler all had big plans for the upcoming season. They all wanted to feature their top-of-the-line cars on the track. These included their largest-bodied, best-selling, and most profitable cars. The American public was still in love with full-sized cars, so the challenge was how to make these big, overweight cars go faster. Everyone realized the advantage of having a light-weight car. Every effort was made to shave pounds wherever possible. Late in 1962, Chevrolet and Pontiac both released some aluminum front-end sheet metal components for their full-sized cars. This small batch of experimental parts set the stage for the 1963 Z-11 Chevy and Super Duty 421 "Swiss Cheese" Pontiacs. Ford stepped up its 1963 program with fiberglass components and a reworked 427-ci engine. Dodge

Pontiac produced only a dozen of its lightweight 1963 Catalinas before the General Motors ban on racing took effect. The large Pontiacs were severely overweight, compared to the lean 1963 Dodges and Plymouths. Drastic measures were taken to get the weight out of these beautiful, but heavy, vehicles. This particular Catalina was campaigned by Packer Pontiac (a Detroit-area Pontiac dealer) and driven by Howard Maseles.

and Plymouth racers also had the option in 1963 of adding aluminum components to their already svelte cars.

Bunkie Knudsen, the former General Manager of Pontiac and the spark plug in revamping that division's cars, was now head of Chevrolet. He loved auto racing and added more voltage to the programs started by Ed Cole and Zora Duntov. Knudsen's love of racing extended to the streets of Detroit, where he often challenged young Turks to the occasional drag race in a Chevrolet Engineering–built Biscayne sedan. He approved the Z-11-optioned Impala for 1963. (It should also be noted that Knudsen also approved Chevrolet's Mystery 427 for NASCAR that year.) These were the first production line cars built by Chevrolet strictly for drag racing. The Z-11 Impalas liberally used aluminum for body panels and bumpers. Under the hood was a stroked 409, increasing the cubic-inch displacement to 427—the maximum legal displacement for NHRA in 1963.

Over at General Motors' Pontiac Division, they were going ahead with plans to build a group of lightweight Catalina sport coupes. Like the Chevys, these cars featured hoods and front

The interior of the 1963 lightweight Catalinas was as stark as a full-size medium-priced sedan could be. Radios and heaters were deleted, but a Hurst Shifter was standard and so was the instrument panel-mounted Pontiac tach.

fenders stamped from aluminum. They also included special exhaust manifolds cast from aluminum and a frame that was drilled with large holes to further reduce weight. The engine was a special 421-ci 420 horsepower V-8. The nickname "Swiss Cheese" was given to these Pontiacs because of their perforated frames. Both of these General Motors cars were far from being practical on the street, due to their high compression ratios, long duration camshafts, and aluminum body panels. Calling them "stock" cars was pure fiction.

Both of these cars were short lived, due to General Motors management's decision to finally adhere to the AMA's 1957 recommendation that the automakers withdraw their support from auto racing. This left Chevrolet and Pontiac competitors with cars to race for 1963, but no further support in the way of free replacement parts. Only a handful of Chevys and Pontiacs were produced and into competitors' hands before the ban went into effect. Also hurt by the ban were the new car dealers who had spent good money sponsoring cars in the hope of expanding their high-performance-hungry customer base.

Ford's 1963 advertising slogan was "Total Performance." In all other forms of racing, Ford could confidently make that

When the lightweight 1963 Catalinas were new, one creative journalist nicknamed them the "Swiss Cheese" Pontiacs. His description derived from the car's frame, which had more holes in it than the Ford sedan in which Bonnie and Clyde had their last shoot-out. Barely visible on the left is the aluminum rear-end center section, used only on the lightweight 1963 Catalinas.

For 1963, Pontiac relied on the same basic 421-ci engine that it had run in 1962. It featured dual Carter AFBs on an aluminum intake manifold and was equipped with unique cast-aluminum exhaust manifolds. These high-performance manifolds were recommended for "drag racing only" because the constant speed of a NASCAR track would generate enough heat to melt the aluminum.

THE BIG ONE!

THE 2nd ANNUAL NATIONAL STOCK CAR CHAMPIONSHIP!

$5,000.00 IN PRIZES FOR STOCK AND COMPETITION CARS!

SATURDAY NIGHT, AUG. 24th AND SUNDAY AFTERNOON, AUG. 25th

THE FASTEST STOCK CARS IN THE WORLD IN THE WORLD'S LARGEST STOCK CAR MEET!

STOCK CAR CHAMPIONS FROM EVERY STATE IN THE UNION ARE COMING IN!

STOCK ELIMINATOR
BOND AWARDS

$2000.00 1st Place
$1000.00 2nd Place
$ 500.00 3rd Place
$ 200.00 4th Place
$ 100.00 5th Place
$ 100.00 6th Place

HUGE SPECIAL 1st, 2nd & 3rd Place Trophies in All Stock Car Classes ... Plus Huge Trophies in Competition and Hot Rod Classes. A Full Program on Saturday Night and Sunday Afternoon.

SPECIAL WINDSHIELD EMBLEM with "PARTICIPANT— 1963 NATIONAL STOCK CAR CHAMPIONSHIP — DETROIT DRAGWAY" to EVERY entry on both days ... in EVERY class, Win or Lose. All classes eligible from Super to Q Stock!—Plus "Hot Rods" and Comp. Cars.

260 BEAUTIFUL TROPHIES AWARDED!

PLUS EXPENSE MONEY!

Tow Money begins at 111 MPH for stock passenger cars during Eliminations. 111 MPH you receive $5.00; at 112 MPH you receive $10.00; at 113 MPH you receive $15.00; at 114 MPH you receive $20.00; at 115 MPH you receive $25.00; and so on, right up the ladder, win or lose!

— ADDED BONUS —

$100.00 Overall Top Speed Ford
$100.00 Overall Top Speed Chevy
$100.00 Overall Top Speed Pontiac
$100.00 Overall Top Speed Ply. or Dodge

—AWARDS SCHEDULE

The Meet will be run on Saturday night, August 24th, and Sunday afternoon, August 25th. Two separate events; two separate Eliminations. Awards listed will be paid half on Saturday, half on Sunday. Example: $1000.00, $500.00, $250.00, $100.00, $50.00 and $50.00 bonds for 1st, 2nd, 3rd, 4th, 5th and 6th on Saturday night, and then the same again Sunday afternoon. Top Speed money will be half Saturday, half Sunday. Tow money will be paid once for your best speed during Eliminations during the entire 2 day meet.

"DYNO DON" NICHOLSON—"MR. CHEVROLET" in his 119 mph '63 Impala!

"HAULING HAYDEN" PROFFITT'S 119 mph 1963 Plymouth from Long Beach, California. Hayden hauls!

DICK BRANNAN from South Bend, Indiana "THE WORLD'S FASTEST FORD!" Dick says, "You're going to have every fast car in the country at that meet. I may not be able to beat all those 'Big Shooters' but I'm sure gonna show 'em what Ford looks like!"

The "OLD RELIABLE" Chevrolet. DAVE STRICKLER and BILL JENKINS. The car that broke the 120 MPH BARRIER!

Young EDDIE SCHARTMAN JR., DON NICHOLSON'S PROTEGE, driving the 118 mph JACK SHAW CHEVROLET!

The fabulous "HORSEPOWER ENGINEERING" DODGE from Pasadena, California. On a vacation trip early this summer he dusted off everyone at the Dragway—Now he MEANS BUSINESS! Can he do it again?

BOB HARROP and the EASTERN RACING TEAM. A team of Red Hot Dodges (119 mph!) From New York, New Jersey, Pennsylvania, and Delaware. ALL CHAMPIONS of the famous YORK U.S. 30 DRAG-O-WAY in York, Pennsylvania.

From Pomona, California, famous BILL "MAVERICK" GOLDEN driving the DRAGMASTER DODGE!

Midwest Chevrolet Pilot LARRY MOODY'S 118 mph Impala!

CHUCK TURNER in the FLOYD FOREN 117mph CHEVROLET!

The pride of the South! MALCOMB DURHAM'S fantastic 118 mph Chevy ... the "STRIP BLAZER" from the NATION'S CAPITAL, Washington D.C.!

From ROYAL PONTIAC— Ace Salesman DICK JESSE driving the POTENT ROYAL TEMPEST!

DETROIT'S CHAMPION! The fabulous GOLDEN COMMANDO PLYMOUTH!

Plus! A FULL COMPETITION SHOW SAT. & SUNDAY!

The BOB FORD INC. RACING TEAM! BILL HUMPHREY & LEN RICHTER in 63½ Fastbacks!

"SMILING GEORGE" DELOREAN'S 118 mph SILVER PONTIAC!

A Huge Stage Show!

DEFENDING NATIONAL CHAMPION JIM WANGERS in the ROYAL PONTIAC!

IMPORTANT:
SINCE SIBLEY ROAD IS TEMPORARILY CLOSED, HERE'S A SHORT CUT TO THE DRAGWAY.

DRAG STRIP
SIBLEY ROAD
ALLEN ROAD
DIX
TELEGRAPH ROAD
PENNSYLVANIA ROAD

SCHEDULE

SATURDAY, AUGUST 24th		SUNDAY, AUGUST 25th	
INSPECTION BEGINS	2:00 P.M.	INSPECTION BEGINS	9:00 A.M.
INSPECTION CLOSES	7:00 P.M.	INSPECTION CLOSES	1:00 P.M.
TIME TRIALS BEGIN	3:00 P.M.	TIME TRIALS BEGIN	9:30 A.M.
TIME TRIALS END	7:30 P.M.	TIME TRIALS END	1:30 P.M.
ELIM. BEGIN	8:00 P.M.	ELIM. BEGIN	2:00 P.M.

— IMPORTANT! —

Pictured above are the early entries only, as of July 25th, 1 month prior to the Championship. Entries were just beginning to pour in from all over the country, as we went to press. We'll leave a little blank spot for the entries received on press day only. We still had 25 days to go!

ONE DAYS ENTRIES

LES RITCHEY owner of PERFORMANCE ASSOCIATES from West Covina, California the FORD KING FROM CAL., with his 117 mph Fastback!

NATIONAL CHAMPION ARNIE BESWICK from Morrison, Illinois with his 117 Catalina and Tempest—A POTENTIAL WINNER!

"GAS RHONDA" from LOS ANGELES! A $7,000.00 — 117 mph Ford!

ONE DAYS ENTRIES

PLUS all of our local favorites "FAST EDDIE" KANTER, McCULLOUGH-RICCI, PACKER PONTIAC, BOB FISHAW, PETE SEATON, RODGER LINDAMOOD—DOZENS OF OTHERS!

There was no place on earth where Super Stocks were held in higher regard than Detroit, Michigan. In 1963 the Second Annual Stock Car Championship was held at Detroit Dragway. The two-day affair drew the best Super Stocks from across the country. In addition to large savings bond awards to the top six cars, bonus cash was paid for top speeds in each brand of car.

In 1963, Hayden Proffitt parked his Chevy and drove a Super Stock Automatic Plymouth. It ran the quarter in 119 miles per hour and was quick enough to win the 1963 Detroit Dragway Stock Car Championship. *Greg Sharp collection*

In 1964, Chrysler introduced its new 426-ci Hemi engine and took a major jump ahead in the battle for the quarter-mile. Here the Oakland, California, based Melrose Missile team of owners Charlie DiBari (left) and Jim DiBari, flank their tuner/driver, Tom Grove. Behind them is the *Melrose Missile IV*. It sits on the Melrose *Launching Pad*, a 1964 state-of-the-art race car transporter. This rig not only transported the race car, but was large enough to carry a spare engine. *Charlie DiBari collection*

claim, but when it came to the drag strip—it came up short. Like the other manufacturers, Ford knew that it had to trim weight—in Ford's case from the Galaxie—to be competitive in Super Stock. In 1963 a standard production line Galaxie fastback with a 427 engine and bucket seats weighed 4,150 pounds. Ford's race version weighed in at 3,480 pounds. This reduction of almost 700 pounds in vehicle weight was accomplished by careful consideration of every component on the car. Ford started with a lighter frame that was used in cars with a six-cylinder engine or 289 V-8. Fiberglass was used for fenders, doors, hood, deck lid, and front inner fenders. The front and rear bumpers and attaching hardware were made from aluminum. The interior was stripped of radio, heater, and clock. A thin rubber mat covered the floor and two smaller-than-standard bucket seats replaced the usually plush Galaxie buckets. The engine was Ford's FE series 427-ci monster rated at 425 horsepower at 6,000 rpm. This is the same engine that was used in NASCAR, with the exception of the dual Holley four-barrels. Since its introduction in 1960 at 352 ci, this engine enjoyed ongoing innovations that improved performance and durability. The only limitation on Ford's Total Performance 1963 lightweight Galaxie was color selection—it had to be white with a red interior.

When the 1963 season began, the Dodge and Plymouth competitors were chomping at the bit. They too had cars with lightweight aluminum components, a trunk-mounted battery, and a stylish hood scoop. Under the hood, the 413 was enlarged to 426 ci. As in 1962, there were two compression ratios to choose from: 11:1 and 13:1. Street racers chose the 11:1 engine, while the serious drag strip competitors selected the 13:1 engine. Transmission choices were still limited to a heavy-duty three-speed and the stout push-button TorqueFlite. There were no limitations on body style, exterior color, or who could buy these cars. Chrysler built enough Dodges and Plymouths for both to legally qualify for Super Stock competition in 1963. General Motors Pontiacs and Chevys and Ford's lightweight Galaxies were relegated to Factory Experimental class competition. The only head-to-head battles against the Mopars were at match races.

With GM officially out of racing, only Ford and Chrysler were left in 1964. Ford contracted with Dearborn Steel Tubing to reconstruct 100 Ford Fairlane sedans into super race cars. On the other side of Detroit, Chrysler engineers revived an engine design that had been shelved a few years earlier—the Hemi.

In 1964, Ford's high-performance Galaxies were too overweight to compete in Super Stock. When equipped with the smaller V-8s, they were relegated to the lower stock classes. If they were equipped with a big block and with additional high-performance factory components and lightweight body panels, they were assigned to the Factory Experimental class, like these two racers.
Greg Sharp collection

Ford realized in 1963 that its full-size passenger cars were too heavy to compete in Super Stock. Its plan for 1964 was to build 100 lightweight Fairlanes powered by Ford's powerful 427 high-riser engine. These cars, named Thunderbolt, were hand-assembled at Dearborn Steel Tubing.

A scant few miles away from Ford's Glass House was a small shop that built custom cars and engineering prototypes for Ford Motor Company. Dearborn Steel Tubing took Fairlane body shells (commonly known as body-in-white) from the nearby assembly plant and converted them into race cars. They stripped the cars down to the bare minimum and added a 427 engine. The missing inboard headlights and blister hood were the visual keys that these cars were not for senior citizens making the Early Bird Special.

On February 11, 1964, Ford Division mailed a letter to all its dealers announcing the availability of the new Ford products for the 1964 drag-racing season. Under Super Stock was listed the Fairlane Thunderbolt. Buyers wishing to purchase one of these cars had to have their order processed by the local Ford District Office. The applicant also had to sign a waiver releasing the dealership and Ford Motor Company from any liability resulting from the use of the car. These cars were also sold without any type of warranty. The 100 Thunderbolts produced turned out to be awesome performers.

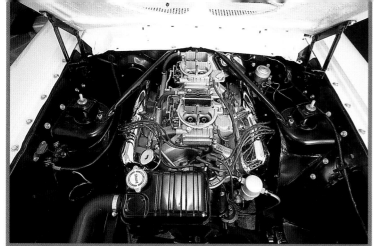

To make room in the Thunderbolt for the 427 engine, the shock towers were cut back and reinforced. All Thunderbolts were equipped with the aluminum high-rise intake manifold with twin Holley four-barrel carburetors. Sitting on top of the carbs was an air box with fresh air hoses connected to the vacant headlight openings.

BELOW LEFT:
To provide clearance for the carburetor's air box on the Thunderbolt, Ford engineers designed a teardrop-shaped bubble hood. The openings in the back of the bubble vent warm air from the engine compartment.

When Chrysler revived its Hemi engine in 1964, it was received like a retired rock star going out on tour again. Everyone, except the competition, wanted to see those big valve covers nestled into a modern engine compartment. The original Hemi was still the favorite engine for Top Fuel dragsters, but the new Hemi offered Chrysler greater exposure of its latest technology through the stock car ranks.

The work on the new Hemi started in 1962, when a request was made to Chrysler's engineering department to develop a new engine that was suitable for oval tracks and drag racing. The Hemi design was the obvious choice for many reasons: valve placement, combustion chamber design, and the ability to use large valves. The 1964 Hemi engine installed in Dodges and Plymouths was all new and only looked like the previous version, last seen in 1958. The new 426-ci Hemi blocks were extremely sturdy with cross-bolted main bearings.

The new Hemi was introduced too late for the 1964 NHRA Winternationals, but it made an auspicious debut at the Daytona 500 that year by taking the first three spots. While

The Thunderbolt's interior was stripped to the basic necessities. Two lightweight bucket seats replace the standard front bench seat. The carpets were removed and a rubber mat was installed in the front floor only, leaving the rear floor bare painted metal. All Thunderbolt interiors were tan vinyl.

Mercury got heavily involved in drag racing in 1964. It also contracted with Dearborn Steel Tubing for a small group of specially built Mercury Comets. With Chevrolet no longer in racing, Don Nicholson switched to Mercury and speced out a Comet station wagon as his personal race car. The Comet Wagon had a shorter wheelbase than the hardtop and more weight over the rear wheels. *James Genat/Zone Five Photo*

NASCAR racers used the sleeker hardtop bodies, the 1964 Hemi drag-race cars were built in the lightest two-door sedan bodies available, the Plymouth Savoy and the Dodge 330. Every weight-saving trick Chrysler had learned while building its quick Max Wedge cars was incorporated into the new factory-built racers. The new Hemi cars were easily distinguished from the Max Wedge cars by their larger hood scoop and by the absence of inboard high beams from the standard quad headlights. It didn't take long for these new Hemi-powered Plymouths and Dodges to start breaking speed and elapsed time records across the nation.

The Hemi engine that won Daytona had a single four-barrel carburetor. The Hemis built for drag racing were equipped with twin four-barrels on a cross-ram intake manifold that was similar in design to the one used on the Max Wedge. Early 1964 Hemis used Carter AFBs. They were soon replaced with a pair of Holley four-barrel carbs. Two compression ratios were available, 11.0:1, which produced 415 horsepower, and 12.5:1, rated

at 425. Only two transmissions were available in 1964, a Hurst-shifted four-speed manual and the push-button TorqueFlite. This would be the last year for the push-button shift.

During the summer of 1964, two Hemi Dodges captured titles in two of the most prestigious races of the year. The Ramchargers won the AHRA Summer Nationals and Roger Lindamood won the NHRA U.S. Nationals with an elapsed time of 11.31 and a speed of 127.84 miles per hour. In the fall of 1964, a Super Stock invitational was held in Cecil County, Maryland. This race drew a large fleet of Dodge and Plymouth Hemis, Ford Thunderbolts, and Mercury Comets. The rules were relaxed, allowing cars that normally competed in the Factory Experimental classes to run against Super Stock entries. Here, the Hemi cars were running elapsed times in the high 10-second range at 130 miles per hour. At the end of the night, the 30-car field had been whittled down to Bud Faubel's Hemi Dodge against "Dyno" Don Nicholson's Comet. Nicholson won and, ironically, took home a Hemi engine as part of his prize package.

Under the hood of the 1965 Super Stock Dodges and Plymouths was the 426-ci Hemi engine. Fitted with aluminum heads, 12.5:1 pistons, and dual Holly carbs on a cross-ram intake manifold, this engine could push one of these squarish sedans down the quarter in 11.25 seconds at 125 miles per hour.

By 1965, Chrysler was the only manufacturer producing cars for the Super Stock class, as Ford had moved on to building Funny Cars. These lightweight A-990 Hemi Dodges and Plymouths were all capable of running the quarter in the low 11-second range with speeds in excess of 125 miles per hour. The only problem was that the fans no longer had a brand to root for—even the most ardent Mopar fans were a little bored. Most of the attention was given to stock-bodied cars in the A/FX class. These cars were no longer hot rods built from a simple mix of factory parts, but custom-built, all-out race cars. In addition to lightweight components, these cars featured altered wheelbases. The bodies were shifted back on the frame for additional traction. These strange looking vehicles were soon dubbed "Funny Cars" and, before long, would be competing in a class of their own.

Stock-bodied race cars were split into two distinct directions in 1966. The stock class was once again dominated by cars manufactured on the assembly line, and the wild Funny Car class got wilder with each custom-built race car. Chrysler wanted to see the cars that it sold in its showrooms winning races on the strip, especially since it released its new Street Hemi engine. Chrysler focused its energies by halting the support of Funny Cars and concentrating on Super Stock teams, like Sox and Martin, who ran a Hemi-powered Plymouth GTX.

Between 1966 and 1970, Detroit was producing some of the hottest machinery ever to rumble down a boulevard. America was basking in the warm golden rays of the Musclecar era, when gasoline had an octane rating higher than its price per gallon. These Musclecars strutted up Woodward Avenue and down Van Nuys Boulevard with a swagger that would scare a professional prize fighter. Street racing was at an all-time high, due in a large part to these factory rocket ships. Unfortunately, the idea of watching these cars run on the strip was not as enticing as it had been a few years earlier. And with the advent of the out-of-control Funny Cars, drag-racing fans had newer and faster heroes. The only blip on the radar screen in the late 1960s happened in 1968, when Chrysler couldn't help itself and produced a handful of custom-built Hemi-powered Plymouth Barracudas and Dodge Darts for Super Stock competition. The Hurst Corporation was contracted to hand-build a limited number of these cars and, like four-years earlier, they were distributed to specific racers. Today, many of these cars survive and are still racing in the Super Stock ranks.

In 1965, Mercury built a limited number of lightweight Comets for the drag strip. The engine powering these cars was either the high-riser 427 or the new SOHC 427. The leading edge of the fiberglass hood has two rectangular intakes for the carburetors. By the end of the year, most 1965 Comets had been modified with an altered wheelbase, straight front axle, and fuel injection—or all of the above.

The stock car drag-racing panorama changed dramatically in 1970, when NHRA introduced Pro Stock as a new class. "Door slammers," as passenger cars were now being called, were back in a big way. Pro Stockers gave the fans a car with just enough changes to make it nastier than a stock version, but with enough of the stock appearance to make for good brand wars. The Pro Stock class was a good idea at the time and as a testament to how good it was, it prevails today as one of the most hotly contested classes.

The new Pro Stock class gave the manufacturers a place to showcase their latest big-block engines in lightweight bodies. The 7.00 pounds-per-cubic-inch rule opened the door for Hemi 'Cudas and 427 Camaros. "Stock" was a bit of a misnomer, as this class allowed engine modifications that included tunnel-ram intakes, fiberglass body components, and large hood scoops. But the cars had to run stock wheelbases and the rear tires had to fit within the original wheel openings. The winner of the first Pro Stock contest at the 1970 Winternationals was Bill "Grumpy" Jenkins, driving a 1968 Camaro. With names like "Dyno" Don Nicholson, Dick Landy, and Arlen Vanke, the list of drivers read like a Super Stock meet from the early 1960s. In the final round, Jenkins, running a 9.99 elapsed time, defeated Sox and Martin's Hemi 'Cuda, which ran a 10.12. Jenkins had the key to Chevrolet Engineering's back door, through which came a constant supply of aluminum 427 blocks and other hard-to-get parts. Jenkins also won the second NHRA Pro Stock race with elapsed times consistently dipping into the nines.

Ford's new Mustang was targeted for a younger male market—like those attending a drag race. By sponsoring cars that were within the financial reach of the average attendee, dealers were able to turn quarter-mile performance into showroom sales. *From the collections of Ford Motor Company*

The NHRA restructured the Super Stock classes to lure production-based cars back into competition. In 1968, Bill Jenkins raced this 396-powered Nova Super Sport. ©1996, NHRA Photographic

The balance of the year was dominated by Sox and Martin's Hemi 'Cuda. "Dyno" Don Nicholson held both ends of the 1970 Pro Stock record, 9.81 seconds at 139.31 miles per hour, and was the only Ford Pro Stock winner in 1970. The popularity of the new Pro Stock class was evident at the May 1970 Super Stock Nationals in York, Pennsylvania, where a 50-car field was ready for eliminations. Ronnie Sox, driving Sox and Martin's Hemi 'Cuda, was the eventual winner, running a best of 9.86 seconds. Sox carried a great deal of momentum into the 1972

In 1970 the NHRA introduced its new Pro-Stock class. This class gave the manufacturers a place to showcase their performance cars. Modifications were allowed, turning these factory sedans into super cars. This class has always been marked by close competition, as can be seen in this race between Ronnie Sox and Butch Leal. *Ron Lewis*

season. By the end of the year, he had won a majority of the races and held the elapsed time record at 9.52 seconds.

There was a major change to NHRA's Pro Stock rules in 1972 that favored compact cars with small-block engines. Jenkins was the first to take advantage of the new rules by building a 331-ci small-block Chevy Vega. It was a killer combination that allowed him to win a majority of the races that year. Jenkins' Vega was also the first Pro Stock car to incorporate a full roll cage. It was not only for protection, but added much needed structural rigidity to the frail unibody construction of the Vega.

Jenkins dominated the early years in Pro Stock, partially because of the rules favoring small-block cars, but mostly because of his brilliant engine-building and tuning skills. Those who couldn't run as fast as Jenkins claimed that he had "secret" components that no one else was able to obtain. Jenkins claimed he wasn't a magician, he just used basic engineering princi-

ples to assemble his engines and construct his cars. For 1972, Jenkins ran a 1972 Vega body with a 331-ci Chevy small-block engine. This combination won many races for him. Between national events, match racing, and product endorsements, Jenkins earned in excess of a quarter-million dollars.

In an article in the December 1972 issue of *Hot Rod* magazine, Jenkins described every major component of his Pro Stock Chevy engine and why he selected it. Jenkins preferred the 327 block with a slight bore to increase the displacement to 331. He had experimented with a 350 engine, but found the performance wasn't any better than the bored 327. On the dyno, Jenkins' little Chevy put out a stout 580 horsepower.

Don Nicholson gained his fame driving Chevys in the early 1960s. In the mid-1960s, he moved on to Mercury, where he drove their Factory Experimental and Funny Cars. With the advent of the Pro Stock class, Nicholson made the switch to Pro Stock and drove Fords. *Ron Lewis*

Pro Stock rules allowed some strange vehicle combinations, including V-8-powered Pintos and the unique Gapp and Rousch *Tijuana Taxi*, a four-door Maverick. The four-door body style offered a longer wheelbase and a weight break. Driving the Pinto in the far lane was Bob Glidden, who would go on to win 10 Pro Stock Championships. *Ron Lewis*

In 1973 a major technical innovation was added to Pro Stock cars that persists today—the Lenco transmission. The Lenco instantly rendered obsolete all other kinds of transmissions by combining planetary gear sets with a mechanical shift linkage. Another big advantage of the Lenco was an unlimited combination of gear sets. While heavy and above average in using up engine horsepower, the Lenco offered a continuous application of torque and no missed shifts.

Throughout the 1970s, the Pro Stock rules were continually adjusted to allow certain weight and cubic-inch combinations. These adjustments led to some cars being raced that, by all accounts, were not sporty or even attractive. Ford Pintos, Chevy Monzas, and other ugly ducklings were now standard fare in Pro Stock. One of the most interesting Pro Stock race cars was the *Tijuana Taxi*, owned by the team of Gapp and Rousch in 1974. It was a four-door Maverick, with a longer wheelbase and a slight weight advantage over the Pinto the team had been running. The years of odd combinations ended in the early 1980s when the Pro Stock formula was simplified to a 2,350-pound minimum weight with a maximum cubic-inch displacement of 500. This rule change increased competition, bumped up speeds, and lowered elapsed times.

In 1975, *Motor Trend* magazine named the new Chevy Monza its car of the year. It was also Jenkins' choice for Pro Stock competition. Dubbed *Grumpy's Toy XII*, Jenkins' Monza featured a much sleeker body than the Vega he had been running. Chevrolet wind tunnel tests confirmed that the Monza had 12 percent less drag than the Vega. Jenkins added two small spoilers to the rear deck to help plant the back end at high speeds. And as he had done in his successful Vegas, Jenkins continued to run the 331 small-block Chevy engine.

While "Grumpy" Jenkins set the early tone for Pro Stock, Bob Glidden became its undisputed king. Glidden's accomplishments in Pro Stock are legendary. In 1972, Glidden was runner-up to Jenkins in the first Pro Stock race he entered. Known best for the Ford Pintos, Probes, Fairmonts, and Thunderbirds he drove, Glidden also successfully raced a Plymouth Arrow in 1979. When he finally retired in 1997 after 22 years as a pro, Glidden had recorded an amazing 85 National Event wins and 10 NHRA National Championships.

Bill "Grumpy" Jenkins is a legend in drag racing, from tuning and racing all kinds of Super Stock and FX cars in the 1960s to his dominance in the Pro Stock class. In 1975 he built and drove this small-block-powered Chevy Monza. The nose-down stance of the car was typical of the Pro Stock cars of the era.

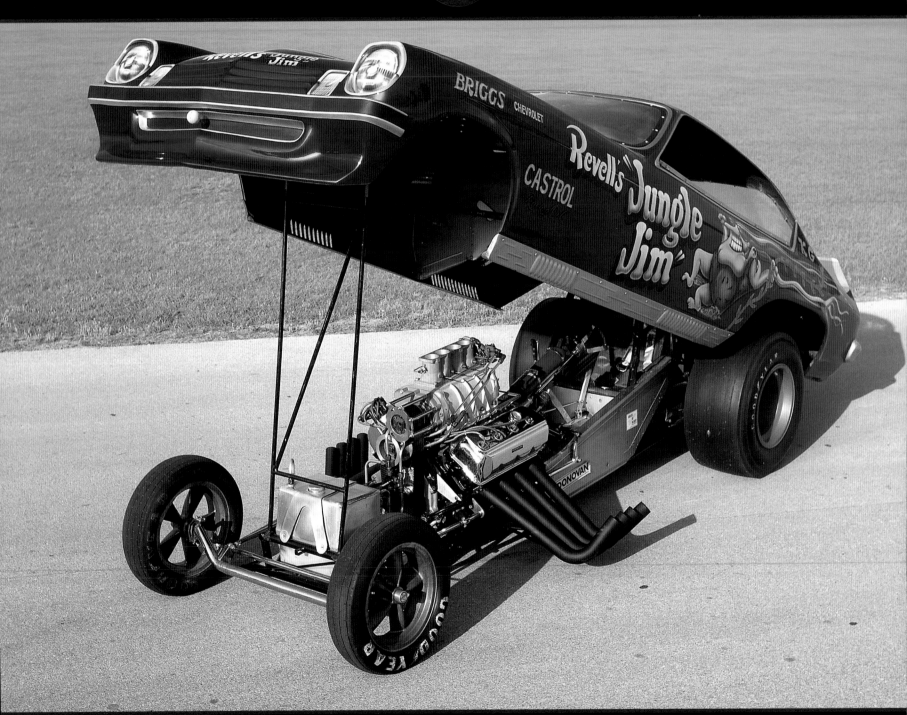

5

Funny Cars

The Super Stock and A/FX wars of the early 1960s bred a new type of race car that would eventually be the most exciting thing on the track—the Funny Car. This new class of car featured a manufacturer brand name for which to root, a supercharged fuel-burning engine, long smoky burn-outs, and out-of-control side-by-side racing—all fan favorites. Funny Cars turned out to be more fun than free beer at an August baseball game.

In 1964 many competitors in the Factory Experimental class began to "adjust" the wheelbase of their cars. They pushed the front and rear wheels forward, effectively moving the body rearward, which relocated the car's center of gravity rearward for better traction. (It has been documented that a few cars running in Super Stock in 1962 had small, but effective, changes in wheel location to aid traction.) In 1965, Chrysler provided race cars with altered wheelbases directly to competitors. The rear axle on these Dodges and Plymouths was moved forward 15 inches, placing the rear wheel at the rear edge of the door opening. The front wheels were moved forward 10 inches, requiring a stainless-steel cross-member. These cars had acid-dipped bodies, plexiglass windows, and fiberglass fenders, hoods, and instrument panels. Race-ready, they weighed in at 2,500 pounds, well under the allowable 3,200-pound limit for Factory Experimental. This allowed the competitors to add ballast for traction. Under the hood was the powerful Hemi engine, now equipped with an Isky roller cam and new aluminum heads. Rated at 425 horsepower, in this form it produced an actual 500 to 600 horses.

Ford Motor Company was heavily involved in all types of automotive racing in 1965. Ford wanted to win every race, no matter what. From Indy to LeMans, Ford had a car and an engine designed to put a blue oval in the winner's circle. For drag racing in 1965, Ford introduced its version of the Chrysler Hemi—the Single Overhead Cam (SOHC) 427. Affectionately called the "Cammer" by Ford enthusiasts, this single overhead cam design allowed it to rev freely and to match or surpass the Chrysler Hemi in horsepower. It was the Holy Grail for which the Ford drag racers had been searching.

One of the most colorful drivers to ever climb into a Funny Car was Jungle Jim Liberman. His on-track antics earned him legions of fans across the country. Wherever he was booked for a match race, it was standing room only, as everyone wanted to see what this superstar of Funny Cars was going to do next.

The mold for Funny Cars was cast in 1965 with the introduction of the Chrysler-built altered-wheelbase Dodges and Plymouths. The relocation of the front and rear wheels forward had the same effect as setting the engine back in the chassis. This rearward weight bias gave the Mopars a clear-cut starting line advantage—so much so that even an amateur driver like Norm "Mr. Norm" Kraus could pull the front wheels off the ground. *Norm Kraus collection*

Ford also made another change to its drag racing program in 1965. It parked the "mom and pop" Thunderbolt Fairlane sedan and installed the big gun Cammer in a Mustang. Released in April 1964, the sporty Mustang had taken the country by storm and Ford wanted to continue that momentum by showcasing it as its premier drag-racing car. The Mustang now had the performance image Ford wanted to associate with youth and drag racing.

While Chrysler built its cars in-house, Ford contracted Holman & Moody in Charlotte, North Carolina, to build its drag-race Mustangs. They chose the sporty fastback, stripped the body of all unnecessary frills (radio, heater, and sound deadener), and installed a sturdy roll cage. Like the Chrysler cars, these Mustangs used fiberglass body components for their light weight. The Mustang's rear wheelwells were enlarged to accept massive 10.00x15 M&H Racemaster slicks mounted on 6-inch wide American mags. Ford wanted to keep the Mustang's sleek proportions within reason and moved the rear axle forward only 2 inches. Special traction bars were added to the 9-inch Ford rear axle. To make room in the engine compartment for the

The 1965 Mopar altered-wheelbase cars soon sprouted injector stacks through the hood, as the owners removed the Hemi's cross-ram intake in favor of fuel injection units. Along with the injectors came the addition of exotic fuel. In 1965 a fuel-injected Dodge Funny Car could run the quarter in 9.5 seconds at a speed of over 140 miles per hour. *Curt Stimpson*

wide Cammer engine, the spring towers were removed and a flat leaf spring replaced each front coil spring.

Chrysler debuted its battalion of Super Stock and A/FX combatants at the 1965 AHRA Winter Championships held in Scottsdale, Arizona. Class designations in the AHRA included Ultra/Stock (U/S) for exotic altered wheelbase factory cars and Super/Stock (S/S) for moderately (2 percent) altered wheelbase cars that looked stock with a minimum weight of 3,200 pounds. The *Melrose Missile* Plymouth was the fastest S/S qualifier, with a time of 11.03 seconds. The team of Sox and Martin was the fastest U/S qualifier at 10.74 seconds driving an altered wheelbase Plymouth.

Only one Ford competitor showed up for the race—Phil Bonner. He qualified his 1964 427-powered Falcon in U/S at 10.83. His brand-new Cammer Mustang was sitting on his trailer—and there it would stay. Ford officials didn't want the untried Mustang to run against the Mopars. They were also a little miffed at Chrysler's severely altered wheelbase race cars, which Ford argued "violated the spirit of the rules." Bud Faubel's Dodge took Top Stock Eliminator at the meet, with an elapsed time of 10.96 at 129.31 miles per hour.

Ford opened its 1965 season with a win at the NHRA Winternationals. Bill Lawton won the A/FX class in his Cammer-powered Mustang with a run of 10.92 seconds and a top speed of 128.20. Later in 1965, Gas Rhonda, driving a Cammer-powered Mustang, set the A/FX record at 10.43 seconds with a speed of 134.73.

Early in the season there was more conflict off-track than on it. Officials from both Ford and Chrysler whined that the other had an unfair advantage because of the way they built their cars. Ford's beef was with the severity with which the wheelbases were altered on the Chrysler cars—the cars looked "funny." Chrysler's main complaint was that Ford used the smaller Mustang instead of its midsized Fairlane, as it had in 1964. The animosity escalated to a point where Ford directed its racers not to compete against any car that would not be legal under NHRA A/FX rules. This included the altered wheelbase Mopars and a few independents running Chevys, which did not qualify as legal A/FX cars under NHRA rules. If a Ford factory competitor were to race an altered wheelbase Mopar, the penalty was a recall of the race car, engines, and spare parts. Match racing was the drag racer's bread and butter in 1965. To be restricted from competing would have had an adverse impact on his income. Chrysler also instituted its own set of restrictions.

To combat Chrysler's altered-wheelbase cars, Ford produced a number of specially built 1965 Mustangs. These cars were hand-built by the Holman and Moody race shop. Unlike Chrysler's altered wheelbase cars, Ford intended to make these Mustangs look more like a production car.

The penalty for an infraction was an end to support—no more free parts. This early-season squabbling between Ford and Chrysler over the "legality" of each other's cars caused track owners to go prematurely gray. Racers began to wonder how they were going to make the next payment on their rig. A Ford racing a Ford, or a Plymouth racing a Dodge, was not going to draw a crowd.

Racers like to race and corporate types like to send memos. Unfortunately racers do not like to read memos, but Chrysler kept sending them. On May 11, 1965, H. Dale Reeker sent a memo to the Chrysler race teams directing them not to use any

Under the hood of the 1965 A/FX Mustang was Ford's silver bullet—the Single Overhead Cam (SOHC) 427 engine. Unable to run the engine in NASCAR competition, Ford focused its 427 efforts on drag racing. To fit the wide SOHC engine into the narrow Mustang engine compartment, the spring towers were eliminated. In 1965, in addition to A/FX competition, this engine was also used in Fuel Dragsters.

exotic fuel. He also told them that they should tell their competitors to run gasoline, too. One week later, Reeker directed all Chrysler competitors not to do wheelies, because it might "damage the cars." I'm sure the competitors were waiting for the let's-put-mufflers-on-the-cars-because-they're-too-loud memo. It wasn't long before the memos stopped and the cold war on paper turned to the hot war on the track. The promoters were now allowed to give the fans the races they wanted to see—Mustang versus Dodge, or Plymouth versus Mustang. Even a few of the A/FX Mercury Comets got into the act.

The 1965 A/FX Comets, built at Bill Stroppe's West Coast shop, were running with the biggest disadvantage because their stock wheelbase was 1 inch longer than that of the Mustang or Mopar. "Dyno" Don Nicholson was the first to take the torch to his Comet by moving the rear wheels forward 10 inches. Now the floodgates were open. Hilborn fuel injection, an item reserved for all-out race cars, was first seen on the Golden Commando's Hemi Plymouth. Before long, all the major Mopar teams were running fuel injection. Soon Nicholson added Hilborn injection to his Cammer engine and then removed the stock front suspension and added a Woody Gilmore straight front axle. Running on gas, Nicholson's Comet ran the quarter in 10.28 seconds at 134 miles per hour. With the addition of an exotic fuel blend, Nicholson became the first Comet driver to break the 10-second barrier, when he ran a 9.91 at 137 miles per hour. Within the year,

In 1966, Mercury set the tone for the next 35 years of Funny Car racing when it contracted for Logghe Stamping to build four race car chassis that would be fitted with a one-piece fiberglass 1966 Comet body. For power they would use the Cammer engine. Because of the way the uniquely rear hinged body opened and closed, the name "Flopper" was used describe Funny Cars. *Pete Garramone*

The Colorado-based team of Kenz and Leslie was one of the lucky four to receive a 1966 Mercury Comet Funny Car. Mercury was smart enough to distribute the four cars it had built to four separate regions of the country. Kenz and Leslie were longtime Ford supporters, and before the Funny Car owned a Ford-powered dragster. *Pete Garramone*

elapsed times dropped one full second and speeds increased by close to 10 miles per hour. It was an exciting time in drag racing.

The rapid changes in 1965 were nothing compared to what was coming in 1966. Late in 1965, Chrysler realized that the outlandish A/FX race cars and match racing was out of step with the exposure they originally wanted from drag racing. The cars the company was sponsoring were no longer representative of the models sitting on the showroom floor at Dodge and Plymouth dealerships. Chrysler decided to put its emphasis back on the Super Stock class. This was due in large part to the pending release of the Street Hemi engine. Chrysler did offer some compensation to those who had been faithfully flying the Mopar flag. Teams wishing to run their 1965 Funny Cars were offered some free parts, machining expenses, and 10 cents per mile for travel. Competitors were also given title to the car. Some corporate strings were still attached: the cars could run fuel, but no blowers. Chrysler competitors were instructed to refuse match races against any blown car. A few of the Funny Car competitors switched to Super Stock and many built all-out match race cars.

Ford Motor Company was fully entrenched for the 1966 Funny Car season. The new Mustangs were no longer based on factory body shells but were full competition models. These new models had elongated front ends and were soon dubbed "long nose" Mustangs. The big news out of Dearborn in 1966 wasn't the Mustang, but the radical Mercury Comet that was being prepared for Funny Car competition. Al Turner led the Mercury racing effort. He collaborated with the Logghe brothers on the body and chassis design for what would become the most sensational and innovative Funny Car ever to leave parallel black streaks on pavement.

In the early 1960s, Ron and Gene Logghe owned a Detroit-area stamping company, where they produced quality parts for the automotive industry. They were also dyed-in-the-wool hot rodders who used a corner of their shop to build race car chassis. Turner approached the brothers about adapting one of their altered chassis for the 1966 Comet Funny Car he had in mind. They made a few sketches and got to work building a total of four cars for Mercury.

The frame was constructed from 1-1/2 -inch and 1-7/8-inch-diameter chrome moly tubing. Coil-over shocks were used on the front and rear. The front axle was tubular, supported by a four-bar suspension, and the 9-inch Ford rear end was held in place with ladder bars. To keep the slicks within the wheel openings, the rear end was narrowed. The brake system consisted of disc units on the rear only. Like an Altered Coupe, the car had its single seat in the center and as far aft as the body would allow.

Powering the Comet was the Ford Cammer fitted with Hilborn fuel injectors. Because the standard Funny Car fuel was now a blend of nitromethane, the compression ratio was dropped from its usual 12:1 to 10:1. Engine upgrades consisted of a Crane cam, Mallory Super-Mag ignition, and custom-made collector-type headers. The headers were soon replaced by dragster-style weed-burner pipes. Don Nicholson received the first car of the four cars built. Nicholson's car was fitted with a four-speed manual transmission. Because of the center seating position, shifting was difficult and soon a C6 automatic was installed.

Ford contracted with the Plastigage Corporation for the custom-built 1966 Comet fiberglass bodies. Ford provided the company with a styling model for its body mold. The body's total weight was 250 pounds, which included the thin plexiglass side windows and windshield. When the cars were painted, the bumpers, grille, and headlights were sprayed silver to correspond to the original factory bright trim. From a distance, these cars had the appearance of a factory stock Comet. On the front

The Funny Car revolution intensified in 1966. Chevrolet fans were happy to see independents like Bruce Larson racing his 1966 Chevelle. Radically altered wheelbase cars were no longer the accepted norm in Funny Car competition. Larson's Chevelle reflects that trend, with a vehicle that looks like a mildly modified production car.

fender of each car, the name "Mercury Comet" was painted in large letters. Painted on the side of Nicholson's factory-sponsored car was *Eliminator I*, while Eddie Schartman drove the Air Lift sponsored *Air Lift Rattler*. Jack Chrisman ran the *GT-1*, which was sponsored by Kendall Oil. The fourth car went to the team of Kenz and Leslie, running out of Colorado. Each of these racers was based in a different geographic region of the country, which meant that fans all across the nation would have a chance to see one of these fabulous new Comets.

Before Mercury introduced the 1966 Comet, Funny Car drivers climbed in and out of their cars through the vacant side glass openings or working passenger doors. These Comets had no working doors and full side glass, with the exception of the driver side door area. For access to the driver seat, the builders decided to hinge the one-piece Comet body at the rear. Hinging a body at the rear wasn't a new idea. At the 1956 NHRA

Instead of a flip-top body, Bruce Larson's all-fiberglass-bodied 1966 Chevelle had a fiberglass front end that would tilt forward or could be completely removed. With the front end removed, the injected 427-ci Chevrolet big-block engine can be seen. Also revealed is the tube frame and forward-mounted Moon fuel tank. The front hinge pillars are the only remaining steel components from the original Chevelle body, and even they have been drilled to reduce weight.

WHEELSTANDERS

One of the things that raised the blood pressure of drag-racing fans was the occasional wheelstand that a race car might pull at the start. Pulling the front wheels a few inches off the ground at the start of a race always looked impressive. It told the fans that the car had an excess of horsepower and a lot of traction. But when the inches grew to feet, it became a serious problem—except for the fans, who loved it. Fans would whoop and holler when one of the cars did a big wheelie. Unfortunately, the wheelstanding competitor would usually lose the round and often broke a lot of parts on a hard landing.

Once the racers saw how much the fans loved the wheelstands, a few competitors traded in their race cars for exhibition vehicles that were intentionally built to do spectacular wheelstands. The track promoters also realized that the wheelstanding exhibitions were fan favorites. Wheelstanding demonstration runs were also less expensive than campaigning a race car. The owners found that they got more money for doing a few moderate speed demonstration runs with the wheels in the sky than they did racing hard against other cars with all four wheels on the track.

The wheelstand is a spectacular phenomenon that happens in drag racing when there is a simultaneous abundance of horsepower and traction. In the mid-1960s, many drag racers capitalized on the demand by fans for cars that could do spectacular wheelstands, like the Hemi-powered *Little Red Wagon*. *Chrysler Historical*

The Little Red Wagon was one of the most famous wheelstanders. It started life as a docile Dodge A-100 compact pickup truck that was going to be campaigned in the Factory Experimental class. Dick Branster and Roger Lindamood—the brain trust of the Color Me Gone Super Stock Dodge—took over a project started by two fellow Detroiters, Jim Collier and Jim Schaeffer. The concept was simple—put a big Hemi engine in the back of a light pickup. A small subframe held the engine, transmission, and rear axle. The truck's front suspension was a stock beam axle. It was the most unlikely of race cars and an even more unlikely wheelstander—that was the hook.

Because the short wheelbase placed most of the weight over the rear wheels, the Little Red Wagon's traction was phenomenal. From the starting line, it could snap the wheels off the ground and carry them clear through the traps. The Little Red Wagon toured the nation, amazing drag-racing fans with its aerial act. It didn't take long for other wheelstanding cars to be built. Soon, races between wheelstanders were taking place to see which one could get to the end of the quarter first, carrying the front wheels all the way.

National Championship Drags, Carl Grimes ran an A/Altered coupe. His 1948 Fiat body was welded together and hinged at the rear of the chassis allowing it to tilt open almost a full 90 degrees. It was natural that the large one-piece Comet body would be hinged at the rear, like the Altereds. This allowed the driver easy entry and exit and gave the crew free access to the engine. The 1966 Comet set the direction for the design of all future Funny Cars—a one-piece fiberglass body hinged at the rear on a tubular race car chassis. Because of the way the body flopped open and closed, these Comets were soon dubbed "Floppers"—a name that endures today.

Along with being innovative, Mercury's newest stable of race cars was also fast. The Comets immediately rewrote the record book by dropping into the eight-second range—cutting a full second off the best previous Funny Car run. At the 1967 AHRA Winter National meet, held at the Bee Line drag strip in Phoenix, Arizona, Nicholson paced the field by running an 8.26 elapsed time at 172.08 miles per hour. His

The interior of Bruce Larson's 1966 Chevelle was fabricated from sheet aluminum. The only interior components from a 1966 Chevelle are the door trim panels and door handles. A large Moon pedal is used for the accelerator, and a small aftermarket steering wheel is placed in front of the single bucket seat.

The 1966 *Drag News* Super-Super Stock Invitational meet was held at New Jersey's Atco drag strip. When this meet was first held a few years earlier, the cars that attended were factory Super Stocks. In 1966 a true Super Stock would not have been competitive against the field of Funny Cars attending.

the DRAG NEWS Super Super Stock invitational championships

SEE ALL THE BIG BOYS IN ACTION INCLUDING:
- SOX & MARTIN
- MAYNARD RUPP
- DARRELL DROKE
- BOB HARROPP
- DON NICHOLSON
- DOUGS HEADERS
- MELROSE MISSILE
- DICK BRANNAN
- ARNIE BESWICK
- PHIL BONNER
- JACK CHRISMAN
- HOUSTON PLATT

ALL THE TOP CARS IN THE NATION ARE HEADED FOR BEAUTIFUL ATCO DRAGWAY FOR THIS ONCE IN A LIFETIME DRAG RACING EXTRAVAGANZA. ONLY DRAG NEWS COULD ASSEMBLE SUCH A SHOWCASE OF STARS IN ONE PLACE AT ONE TIME....HOPE TO SEE YOU THERE!!!

FIRST ROUND INJECTED WIN PAYS: **$1000.** SECOND ROUND INJECTED WIN PAYS... **$750.** FIRST ROUND SUPERCHARGED WIN PAYS **$1000.**

SCHEDULE:
Gates Open ...4 P.M.
Time Trials...5 P.M.
Entries Close...8 P.M.
Races Begin...8:30 P.M.
(and end early)

ATCO DRAGWAY   ATCO, NEW JERSEY
LOCATED 4 MILES DOWN JACKSON RD. TAKE THE NEW JERSEY TURNPIKE TO EXIT 4 - EAST ON 73.

WEDNESDAY NITE ——— AUGUST 3 RD

competitor in the final run for Unlimited Stock Eliminator was Ed Schartman in another Comet.

All earlier Funny Cars were now obsolete. The only way anyone could compete with the new Mercury Comet was to build a car in the same fashion (tube chassis and fiberglass body) or add a blower—and most did both. The new field of Funny Cars no longer had the altered wheelbase proportions of the 1965 models. They, like Mercury's new Comets, looked more like passenger cars. Before long, even some of those would be modified with the addition of a blower or by sawing the roof off. For the fans, every trip to the drag strip was an adventure in automotive excess, a chance to see the latest fad in Funny Cars.

By 1967, Top Fuel dragsters were losing their grasp on the fans. Instead, Funny Cars were becoming the big drawing card

for track owners. Funny Cars were fast, and each run was on the raggedy edge of control. Match races were booked from coast to coast. In 1967, Orange County International Raceway, in Southern California, held a Manufacturers' Championship. At that time, in addition to a full fleet of manufacturers' bodies in competition, the Funny Cars were running a good mix of engines—Ford Cammers, big-block Chevys, Chrysler Hemis and even a few Pontiac powerplants. This diverse mix of engines and corporate bodies allowed promoters to play to the natural automotive biases of race fans. Track announcers earned their pay by whipping the crowd into a frenzy over a match race featuring a Ford versus Chevy, or a Dodge versus Mercury.

A true drag racer will race anything with wheels. In 1967 many dragster owners and drivers were switching to Funny Cars—that's where the money was. That same year, this new class of racing became a permanent fixture at NHRA national events. The winner of the first Funny Car championship at the 1967 NHRA Nationals was Doug Thorley driving Doug's Headers Corvair. Funny Cars were now recognized as something other than a flash in the pan. The big money in Funny Cars was not at the NHRA or AHRA National Events, but in touring the nation running match races. Funny Cars had become an integral part of the drag-racing spectacle.

In the early 1970s, Pomona was the only West Coast track holding large NHRA national events. Many of the original West Coast tracks had fallen into disrepair and needed a shot in the arm to draw the race-hungry crowds. "We had an interesting situation with Orange County and Irwindale," said the late Steve Evans, who, along with Bill Doner, managed most of the West Coast tracks in the 1970s. "We were in the same market, but we didn't have an NHRA national event. We had to do other things."

Ohio native Ed Schartman drove the *Air Lift Rattler* Mercury Comet/Cyclone Funny Car in 1966 and 1967. This is the 1967 version, which was painted dark blue. At this time, roof hatches were not standard equipment on Funny Cars. Drivers either climbed out of the open side windows or waited until the body was opened. Aerodynamics were coming into play in 1967, and a small front spoiler was added on the front bumper bearing the Mercury name. *Author collection*

Being competitive in the Funny Car class in 1968 required a full race chassis, a supercharged engine, and a fiberglass replica body. New car dealers, like Grand Spaulding Dodge, which, a few years earlier, would order a race car from the factory, now had to have its cars built by a specialty race car shop. The cost of going fast was escalating. Here, the Grand Spaulding Dodge Charger Funny Car is being towed through the pits following a run by a factory-produced Dodge Charger. *Norm Kraus collection*

RIGHT:
In 1969 every Funny Car had a flip-top body. Most, like the Grand Spaulding Dodge Charger, opened from the front. In the background is Arnie Beswick's 1969 GTO. Its body was hinged at the front. *Norm Kraus collection*

Those "other things" required lots of Funny Cars and *lots* of promotion. "Bill Doner and I were the fathers of the really big Funny Car shows," recalled Evans. "I remember the first time we ran 32 Funny Cars at Irwindale. Oh God, did we jam that place!" Evan and Doner's shows started small, with 16 cars. Then it went to a 32-car show and then 64 cars. Many of the cars competing were touring cars. The fans had their favorites and those were usually the ones that cost the most to book. The cost of booking a Funny Car in the 1970s ran between $750 and $3,500. Most cars ran for the guarantee. If there was a purse for the winner, it was small. Many times a purse was offered to a local car in lieu of appearance money. The cars ran round-robin Chicago style, where there are two rounds of racing, with the two low elapsed time winners returning for the final.

Funny Car technology didn't change much between 1966 and 1969. The Logghe chassis under Mr. Norm's 1969 Dodge Charger Funny Car was very similar to the one under Nicholson's 1966 Comet. Logghe's side frame rails were a ladder style and the front and rear suspension relied on coil-over shocks. Unlike 1966 Funny Cars, all of the Funny Cars in 1969 were supercharged. *Norm Kraus collection*

FAST AND FRANTIC WITH FLAIR

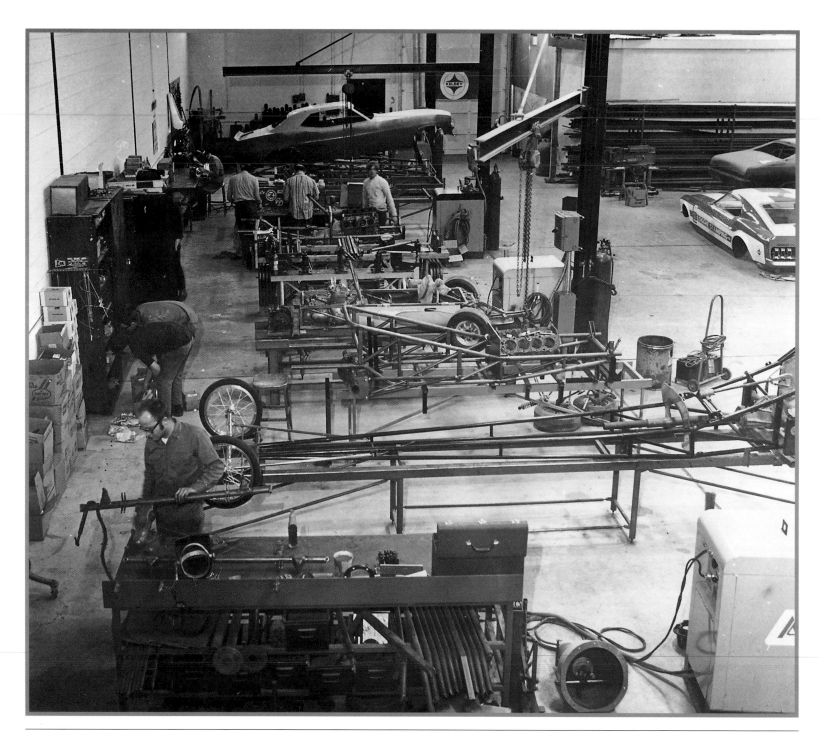

Logghe Stamping Company was the Midwest's home for race car chassis and parts. In addition to building components, it constructed complete cars. Seen in the foreground is a dragster chassis under construction. Behind it is a Funny Car chassis fitted with a bare block. In the background is a Dodge Challenger Funny Car body and off to the right is a Ford Mustang body. *John Logghe collection*

Funny Car match races in 1969 brought the same level of excitement from fans as the Super Stock match races six years earlier. Ford versus Dodge was a big draw especially when two high-profile racers like the Mr. Norm Dodge Charger faced off against the Stone, Woods, and Cooke Mustang. *Norm Kraus collection*

The promotions for drag racing were primarily done on radio—rock 'n' roll radio. "We were real aggressive on our Funny Car shows," said Evans. "We had some really clever ads, got a lot of people excited, and we put some bodies in the stands." Doner and Evans were unique because they wrote, produced, and voiced their own radio commercials. They were pitching to young fans in their late teens and early twenties. Doner and Evans knew their market. "The 'Fox Hunts' were huge—I invented that," boasted Evans. On Fox Hunt night, all ladies got into the track for free on the spectator side. They had to pay for a pit pass, but there was usually a long line of guys with extra pit passes hanging around the gate to the pits. "Sex sells," exclaimed Evans. "I don't care what business you're talking about." The Fox Hunts were imitated all over the country. Rock 'n' roll bands were also showcased after a race with a radio promotion that blared, "Come boogie in the trick traction compound!"

The promotions continued to get bigger with an advertised 100 Funny Car show, although it's questionable whether 100 operating Funny Cars ever actually appeared at any track at one time. One of the highlights of these big Funny Car shows was the lineup of cars on the track prior to the race. The intent was to have them all idling, creating a wall of sound—rocking and rolling nitro-burning engines. Unfortunately, many of the cars wouldn't fire. To make it look as if they were running, crew members would shake the body prop. Burn-out contests were

another part of the spectacle. The promoter would ante up an additional $500 to the driver judged by the fans to have done the best burn-out. Steve Evans recalled one memorable night at Irwindale when "Big" Jim Dunn literally "smoked" the competition. "Dunn smoked the tires all the way to the finish line, turned around, and had his kid Mike pour some more water down. Then he came back *up* the race track, smoking the tires!" Dunn was instructed not to do that again.

Jumping cars and trucks with a motorcycle was not an unusual stunt in the 1970s, but jumping Funny Cars was. One night at Orange County, they had arranged to have a motorcycle, with a large kite-like wing attached, jump over a line of Funny Cars. Tommy Ivo waited to be the last car at the end of the line. "Ivo wanted a new body for his race car so he waited and waited until he could be at the end of the line. Sure enough, the motorcycle clipped Ivo's car and we had to buy him a new body," recalled Evans.

Don Schumacher was one of the first stars of the Funny Car class. He grew up in the Chicago area and took his first pass down

In 1971, Shirley Muldowney parked her twin-engine dragster and got behind the wheel of this Mustang Funny Car. In her first race in Lebanon Valley, New York, Muldowney showed the world what an excellent driver she was by winning the event. *Shirley Muldowney collection*

Shirley Muldowney drove Funny Cars for four seasons before moving on to Top Fuel. During her time in Funny Cars, she was injured in more than one fiery accident. Many of the safety measures in today's Funny Cars were developed as a result of what these early pioneers encountered behind the wheel. *Shirley Muldowney collection*

In 1970, Mickey Thompson was heavily involved with Ford Motor Company. He asked Nye Frank, one of the craftsmen in his shop, to build this 1970 Mustang Mach I Funny Car. This car was unusual because the chassis was a monocoque design with an aluminum lower tub similar to an Indy car. Because of the unique design, only the top portion of the body opened. This car was powered by a supercharged Ford Boss 429 engine.

a drag strip in a 1963 Oldsmobile Starfire. "I went to a drag strip in Gary, Indiana, called U.S. 30, and got beat with my stocker the first time—I didn't like that," confides Schumacher. The Olds was Schumacher's everyday transportation. Up until that race, he had never even changed a set of spark plugs. Schumacher was hooked on drag racing. He started to strip everything he could out of the car to get the weight down. That winter, he ordered a custommade set of fiberglass body components so he could go faster. The following year, Schumacher built his first Funny Car with the help of R&B Automotive in Kenosha, Wisconsin. R&B was owned by Dennis Rolaine and John Buttera. They had made a name for themselves in the area by first repairing race cars and eventually building them. The car that R&B built for Schumacher was a Dodge with an injected Hemi that he ran for two years. The transition from the Olds to a Funny Car was dramatic. "You don't necessarily notice the horsepower," says Schumacher. "You notice the speed! Going 150 made my hair stand up on end and I got the biggest charge out of it."

In 1966, Schumacher contacted Butch Leal about buying a brand-new Logghe car he was selling. Schumacher came out to California to pick up the car and took it back to Chicago. Late in 1966, he added a supercharger and ran it through 1967 with

the help of John Hogan as his crew chief. In the winter of 1967, he came to California and set Funny Car records at every race track on the West Coast. Schumacher also ran that car at both NHRA and AHRA National meets. "When I came to California is when I started to mature in the sport," says Schumacher. "I remember saying to myself, you know, if Don Garlits can make a living at this, then so can I."

In 1970, Schumacher called his old friend John Buttera and asked him to build a new Funny Car. Buttera had moved from Kenosha to the West Coast to refine his car-building skills with Mickey Thompson. After working for Thompson and some of the other greats in the race car business, Buttera moved into his own shop. The Funny Car that Buttera built for Schumacher was the most advanced to date. It had an independent front suspension with components that were artfully machined by Buttera. A blown Hemi built by Ed Pink was installed. Upon completion, the car was loaded onto a trailer and taken to nearby Orange County Raceway for a shakedown. It was a Saturday night, in late August, and all the big West Coast names in Funny Car racing were there. Orange County Raceway had posted a $5,000 bond for the first Funny Car to break into the six-second range, and every Funny Car driver was trying to take that money home. Schumacher's first pass was only to half-track to make sure the car was stable. On the next pass, Schumacher's plan was to go to the lights. That pass clocked an elapsed time of 6.93 and Schumacher collected the money. From there, he went directly to Indianapolis for the U.S. Nationals, which he won and received the Best Engineered award for his Buttera-built Funny Car.

Don Prudhomme switched from Top Fuel Dragsters to Funny Cars in the early 1970s. In 1973, John Buttera built him this car, which was similar to a car he had built for Don Schumacher. Originally sponsored by Carefree gum, Prudhomme picked up the Army sponsorship in 1974.

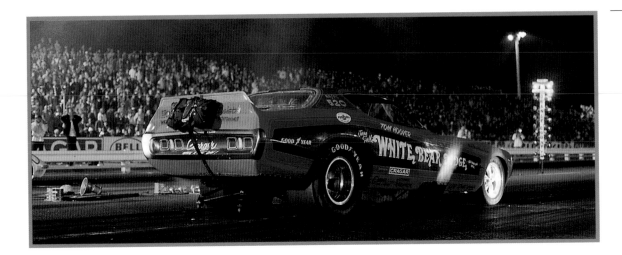

Schumacher admits that winning the 1970 Nationals was his biggest thrill in Funny Car racing. He gives most of the credit to his car builder. "John Buttera was an incredible craftsman and an innovator in the sport," says Schumacher. "I was fortunate enough that when I ordered my first car, he was on his own." Schumacher's success brought a lineup of future legends to Buttera's door to order cars. In the early 1970s, Buttera was the king of the Funny Car chassis business.

Schumacher ran that car for two years and then in 1973, he operated a three-car team of Buttera-built Funny Cars sponsored by the Stardust Hotel. Soon after, Wonder Bread took over the sponsorship of all three race cars and a show car. "The reason Wonder Bread came on board wasn't to advertise to spectators," recalls Schumacher, "it was to motivate their truck drivers. Their drivers were the ones who really sold the bread to grocery stores. By working with the store managers, they got the bread moved from the lower shelf to eye level. It was very successful for them." One of Schumacher's most memorable moments came when he raced in England. "I sent my independent front suspension car to England and ran it under the Stardust name." The English crowd loved the Funny Cars and freely showed its appreciation. When Schumacher backed up from doing his burn-out, he could hear the roar of the crowd over the sound of his engine. The Funny Car frenzy carried over to the hotel where Schumacher was staying. He was treated like a visiting rock star. "At the hotel, I was another Robin Hood," chimes Schumacher. "It got so crazy they had to shut the switchboard down."

Even Jungle Jim's Vega Funny Car had a Chrysler Hemi engine. By the early 1970s, the Hemi had become the mainstay in Funny Car racing. The long header pipes were required to get the exhaust gases out past the body side.

Shirley Muldowney ran Funny Cars from 1971 to 1973. The very first event she entered was a Saturday night show at Lebanon Valley, New York. Muldowney proudly exclaims, "Everybody was there, from Prudhomme to the Ramchargers, and I won! I blew everybody off—it was very impressive." The car she drove was a Mustang she bought from Connie Kallita.

As it turns out, that Mustang was the only "used" race car she has ever run. Every car prior and subsequent to that car has been a new car built for her. "That Mustang was the most ill-handling car you ever saw in your life," recalls Muldowney. "But I wound up running faster and quicker than Kallita [the previous owner] ever did!" Before getting behind the wheel of the Funny Car, Muldowney drove a twin Chevy-engined dragster that her husband, Jack Muldowney, built. Shirley freely admits that she used Funny Cars as a stepping stone to Top Fuel. "It was the most dangerous time in the history of that class," Muldowney recalls. "I ran some great runs, I beat some great people, but I also had some wicked, *wicked* fires." Muldowney survived four serious fires while driving Funny Cars. Funny Car fires in the 1970s were commonplace. Many of the safety features found today in a modern Funny Car, such as onboard fire suppression systems, had not been invented. Also, many of the cars were built on a shoestring, and corners were cut to make it to the track and run fast. In addition, technical inspections at some match race venues were not as stringent as they should have been, in an effort to get a large field for the show.

One of the most colorful legends of Funny Car racing is "Jungle Jim" Liberman. You could count on one hand the number of National events he won, but Liberman had so many bookings for match races, he had to run a second car with another driver. Along with Jungle Pam, they made an interesting pair. She brought sex appeal to the show and he brought a full bag of everything else. "He once told me," says Shirley Muldowney, 'You drive like a man.' You can read a couple of things into it, but I considered it a compliment." Jungle was unpredictable and that's what everyone liked. "Liberman got a little goofy, he led a wild life, there's nothing saintly about the guy," says former NHRA Director of Competition and current NHRA Vice President Steve Gibbs. But Gibbs also experienced a different side to Liberman.

In 1968, Gibbs was running the Fremont drag strip. The drag strip was in the process of changing hands, and the new owners didn't want to start racing until the following year. A race had been scheduled and many of the big Funny Car racers of the day were there for the event, including Jungle. The new owners gave Gibbs the go ahead to run the race as scheduled. The cars ran on Saturday, but the Sunday portion was rained out. Gibbs, now out of a job, had to pay all the expenses for the weekend with only half the gate. He explained to the racers what kind of money he had and the financial obligations that

Anyone who ever met Jungle Jim Liberman or saw him race has a story about the man. He was the original King of Funny Cars. His on-track antics kept the fans entertained and the competitors confused. He received so many bookings that he ran a duplicate car with another driver to make all the dates.

needed to be resolved. "I could only pay them 50 cents on the dollar. I explained to them that was all I had and I was out of a job," says Gibbs. "Some grumbled and griped as they packed up and went home—it was a miserable damn day." At 5 P.M. Gibbs received a call from Liberman. "Come down to the hotel where we're staying, we need to see you." Gibbs expected another round of bitching and moaning from the drivers but went to the hotel anyway. Once there, Jungle said to him, "We know it's a bad deal, we know you tried and have been fair to us, maybe this will help you through it." He handed Gibbs an envelope with between $3,000 and $4,000 in cash—the racers had passed the hat. "For the racers to give money to a track manager . . . I mean, I just get goose bumps thinking about it," says Gibbs. Gibbs is confident that Liberman was the one who pulled it together. "I could never ever have a bad word to say about Jim Liberman," says Gibbs. "And if there was ever anything I could do for him in my position, I would always do it. There was obviously a real human side to him." Jungle Jim Liberman was killed in September 1977, not on the track, but on the street driving a Corvette. Liberman got caught up in a wild lifestyle and took some bad turns, but the many racers who knew him said he was a fascinating individual with an abundance of raw talent for driving, building, and promoting Funny Cars.

The legacy that Jungle Jim Liberman left behind for both racers and fans was the great show he put on. Present-day Funny Car Champion John Force has stepped up to fill Jungle's shoes. While on an East Coast tour in the late 1970s, Force was booked into New Jersey's Old Bridge Township Park. Vinnie Napp, the owner, said to Force, "I booked you in here for a reason. Jungle Jim's dead—he was our star." Napp put on races every Wednesday night called "Vinnie's Night of Thrills." It was everything from truck crushes, to giant robo monsters picking up junk cars, to drag racing 100 Funny Cars. Napp then told Force, "I think you're my next Jungle Jim. Jim's gone and he was our crowd draw. It will take years, but I can turn you into Jungle Jim." Napp told Force that with a good announcer in the tower and long burn-

outs on the track, he didn't have to win races. Napp would also rely on Force taking over Jungle's "wild man" routine of yelling and screaming with the press. Force also toured the same East Coast tracks that Liberman used to frequent. While in Pennsylvania, Force happened to stop into a small hamburger stand, and, like Gibbs, Force was treated to another page of the Jungle Jim story. "It was a 'mom and pop' place and there on the wall was a picture of Jungle Jim," says Force. "I asked the old guy who was the owner if he knew him." The man replied that Liberman used to come in quite often and get a hamburger and a milk shake. He confessed to Force that Liberman was the nicest guy in the world and would always leave a good tip. The owner went on to explain

that one night Liberman took the race car off the trailer and fired it up in the diner's parking lot.

Rising to be the multiyear Champion of the Funny Car class didn't come easily for Force. "I've got a lot of admiration for him," says Gibbs. "John came from nothing—nobody handed him a stack of money." Gibbs was in a position in the sport to see the development of Force's career. "There was a period when you almost hated to see him coming. You knew it—leakers." Leakers are the marginally funded Funny Car teams that show up at events and consistently leak oil on the track. "But you have to work with those guys. We've got guys out there today who are leakers, some of them will always be leakers, but every once in a

while you're going to get one who will get the right break, get the right help and money, and will be your next star."

The evolution of the Funny Cars from a modified passenger car to all-out race car came at a time when wild innovation was part of drag racing. Soon, showmanship took over and the Funny Car proved to be drag racing's headline act. They were fast, loud, and so dangerous that they often burned to the ground. Funny Cars were legitimized when Top Fuel drivers such as Don Prudhomme, Connie Kalitta, Tom McEwen, and Tommy Ivo joined their ranks and became legends in the class. From side show to main attraction, Funny Cars have endured and grown into drag racing's hottest ticket.

6

Coupes, Roadsters, Gassers, and Altereds

D rag racing's roots are firmly embedded in the dry lakes. This was apparent in the February 1953 issue of *Hot Rod* magazine, when a set of six classes was outlined. These drag-racing classes were based on the types of cars that most frequently ran on the dry lakes. Of those six classes, four were designated for Coupes, Sedans, and Roadsters—traditional Southern California hot rods. The other two classes were for Stock cars and Dragsters. These hot rod classes were further broken down by modifications and type of fuel. By 1954 these rules were further defined, but most of the classes were still designed for Coupes, Roadsters, and Sedans.

Coupes and Sedans were split off into their own class, and so were Roadsters. The reason for this separation by body style was the decided aerodynamic advantage that the roadster bodies had over the bulkier coupes and sedans. In the early 1950s, the Coupe and Roadster classes were further broken down into three categories: gas-powered street machines, fuel-burning mildly modified cars, and highly modified versions that burned fuel.

Street classes were designed for the average hot rodder who wanted to take his coupe or roadster out to the drags. The cars were required to run service station pump gasoline only—no aviation gas. Engines had to be in the stock location and a conventional transmission had to be run. Quick-change rear ends were allowed. Cars in these classes were also required to have stock fenders, hood, grille, and an upholstered interior—no gutting was allowed. Mild customizing was permitted, which included chopped tops. If the modifications were too radical, the cars were bumped into a higher class. The street coupes and sedans were split into three classes, all calculated on cubic inches to weight. The class designation was painted on the coupe or sedan's window or body side: A/G, B/G, or C/G, preceded by a registration number. Like the coupe and sedan class, the street roadsters were designated A/R, B/R, or C/R.

In 1959, when the *Walt's Puffer II* Fiat ran at its first NHRA U.S. Nationals, there were only a few rules governing the cars in the class. An automotive body had to be run with its original grille. The top could be chopped, but the overall contour of the body had to remain unaltered. Because of the short wheelbase and loosely interpreted rules, the Altered class was one of the most exciting to watch.

roadsters were designated A/H, B/H, and C/H. All classes were calculated on the ratio of cubic-inch displacement to weight. The addition of a supercharger bumped the car up one class. The Fuel class allowed the drivers with street roadsters to experiment with fuel additives. This was the steppingstone to the Modified or Competition class.

Highly modified coupes and sedans were placed into the Competition class and highly altered roadsters were placed into the Modified roadster class. This was an open Fuel class that allowed the competitors to run anything in their engines that would support combustion. Engine placement was up to the competitor and many cars were rear engined. Transmissions and interiors were not required. Fenders were not allowed, but streamlining forward of the cowl was permitted. Tops could be chopped to allow a minimum of 5 inches of windshield. Soon roadsters in this class would be running without windshields, and coupes would be severely chopped with slanted A-posts that still maintained the 5-inch minimum

Two roadsters blaze off the line at San Diego's Paradise Mesa drag strip in 1955. While the drivers do have helmets, neither car is equipped with a rollbar. *Don Cox*

Addition of fuel—any fuel other than pump gas—bumped the cars up into the Fuel class. Fuel class cars were required to run under the same body and interior rules as the Street class. Engines were allowed a 20 percent (of the total wheelbase measurement) set back and the transmissions were only required to have two forward gears. The three Fuel coupe and sedan classes were designated A/F, B/F, and C/F, and the Fuel windshield. The competition coupes were designated A/C, B/C, or C/C, and the modified roadsters were designated A/M, B/M, or C/M. Cars with superchargers were bumped up a class and those cars that in some way violated the spirit of the rules were moved into the dragster class.

Throughout the 1950s and 1960s, class designations continued to change as the cars evolved. One of those changes was the separation of Light and Heavy coupes. The class was split into the Light Coupe class for cars built between 1929 and 1934 and Heavy Coupes for those 1935 and later. Every sanctioning body had its own classification rules and so did many of the tracks. During the formative years of drag racing, classes changed as rapidly as the cars were modified.

On the West Coast, old roadsters and coupes were plentiful, since they had never had to face the ravages of winter weather. Because of their abundance, they were also inexpensive. An aspiring racer could easily build a roadster or coupe on a budget. Tony Nancy was a West Coast youngster who, in 1956, built a modified roadster. Nancy, who would go on to build three roadsters for the drags, had been introduced to drag racing by friend Tom Sparks. Sparks successfully ran a Willys coupe with a blown flathead. One day he mentioned to Nancy that the engine would run a lot faster in a lightweight roadster. Sparks suggested that Nancy build a roadster and he would let him use the blown flathead out of his coupe.

Without too much trouble, Nancy found a 1929 Ford body and a 1932 Ford frame. He gutted the body and mounted it on the 1932 frame. He lightened the frame and many of the chassis components by drilling holes in them. He installed Sparks' supercharged flathead set back in the chassis. The interior was fitted with sheet aluminum. Nancy trimmed the single bucket seat and crafted a tonneau cover. Running on 50 percent nitro, Nancy broke strip and class records just about everywhere the roadster ran along the West Coast. Along the way, Nancy's roadster even beat a few dragsters for Top Eliminator titles. After two years, 130 trophies, and the cover of the December 1957 issue of *Hot Rod* magazine, Nancy sold this car and started construction of another roadster.

Nancy's second roadster was built more like a race car than a hot rod. It had a custom-built chassis and an overhead valve engine. Kent Fuller built the chassis. His shop was in the same complex as Nancy's interior trim business. At that time, Fuller was also building chassis for Tommy Ivo. Ivo had been successfully running Buick overhead V-8s in his dragsters. He was introduced to the Buick by Max Balchowski, a West Coast sports

Drag racing's dry lakes roots can be clearly seen in this 1934 Ford coupe. The giveaways are the extremely chopped top with slanted A pillars and the smoothed nose. For the mid-1950s, this car was one of the more finely detailed examples. *Don Cox*

The SCTA (Southern California Timing Association) was the principal group that timed dry lakes cars. They also timed drag-racing events as the popularity of drag racing grew. Here, the starter, with flag in hand, is talking to the driver of this 1932 roadster as the two in the timing trailer/tower casually watch. *Don Cox*

This 1934 Ford coupe is more typical of the average drag racer in the early- and mid-1950s. The money is in the engine. Topping the flathead are three Stromberg carbs and a set of aluminum heads. The front fenders and hood have been stripped off and the rear fenders have been bobbed. The exhaust is a simple piece of flex pipe visible behind the front tire. By the looks of the three trophies on the running board, old "Hose Nose" must have known a thing or two about drag racing. *Don Cox*

Part of the classification process was obtaining an accurate weight of the car. Here, NHRA officials roll a Model A coupe up onto the scales. Once the weight was determined, it would be factored against the engine's displacement to determine the class in which the car would run. *Don Cox*

car builder and racer, who was a big proponent of the Buick V-8. With Balchowski's help, Nancy built an injected 450-ci Buick engine for his roadster. The body was a 1929 roadster with several modifications. The cowl and rear deck were built out of aluminum by Phil Remmington. And as Nancy had with his first roadster, he trimmed the interior and tonneau cover. The chassis was painted black and the body was painted the same shade of orange as his previous roadster. Painted prominently in white on the door was what would become Nancy's trademark—22 Jr.

Now running on gas, Nancy's roadster quickly set the track record at San Fernando with a run of 10.74 seconds at 130.57 miles per hour. The editors at *Hot Rod* magazine again recognized

In 1957, Tony Nancy ran this Model A roadster, seen here in the staging lanes at San Fernando Drag Strip. The hood has been removed, exposing the flathead engine, which has been set back in the 1932 Ford chassis. Tom Sparks built the blown fuel-burning flathead for Nancy.
Dan LaCroix collection

Nancy's craftsmanship by shooting his car for the cover of their April 1960 issue. Later in the year, Nancy added a blower to the Buick engine. In February 1961, he competed at the NHRA Winternationals, where he ran in the A/Roadster class and was defeated by the Pennington-LeSage Chrysler-powered entry. NHRA still maintained three classes for roadsters—Roadster, Street Roadster, and Modified Roadster—in 1961, but they were all required to run on gas.

In the early 1960s, a modified roadster was nothing more than a dragster with a roadster body. In 1962, Nancy moved into the Modified Roadster class with a brand-new car that, like his others, was so spectacular that *Hot Rod* magazine shot it for its August 1962 cover. "It's like you reach a plateau," says Nancy. "You reach a spot where you need to make a change to go faster—more spectacular." Nancy took the blown Buick engine out of his A/Roadster and started construction on his new

Part of the fun of going to the drags is hanging out in the pits with your friends. The truck on the left was owned by Tom Sparks, engine builder for Tony Nancy's roadster. *Dan LaCroix collection*

Modified Roadster. "I decided that I'd build a Modified Roadster. It would be sleeker and lighter, and everything was going to be a little bit better." The frame that Nancy had built had a 102-inch wheelbase, as long as many of the era's dragsters. The body, painted in 1958 Lincoln Matador Red by Dean Jeffries,

INSET: With a wisp of smoke off the rear tires, these two roadsters take on a drag strip in Kansas in 1954. The 1932 on the right is running an Oldsmobile V-8 while the red Model T in the left lane is running a flathead with a beautiful set of headers. Even though the car on the right was street driven, the driver has opted to remove the windshield for competition. *Don Cox*

When Tony Nancy decided to build a new race car, he had Kent Fuller make the chassis. Here Nancy, on the left, and Fuller discuss the front suspension. *Kent Fuller collection*

was a fiberglass copy of a 1923 Ford built by Cal Auto. "I built an aluminum cover over the top of it, so that it looked racy," says Nancy. Because of its dragster-like underpinnings, Nancy sat further back and lower than most of his counterparts in the Modified Roadster class. Just like his other cars, Nancy's Modified Roadster would be fast right out of the box. Within a matter of weeks, Nancy had set the track records at San Fernando and Lions. Times for his Modified Roadster were in the low nine-second range at speeds of 170 miles per hour.

LEFT:
While waiting in the staging lanes to run, the owner of this 1932 coupe has jumped up on one of the slicks to watch the action on the track. In 1960, when this photo was taken at Detroit Dragway, 1932 Ford bodies and frames were plentiful and inexpensive. The addition of a Corvette engine with six two-barrel carbs made an excellent combination for the strip. *James Genat/Zone Five Photo*

Roadsters and coupes each had their own followings at the strip. Some fans loved the roadsters and others loved the coupes. One of the coupe classes that became an overwhelming favorite of closed body fans was the Gas Coupe class, which the fans came to know simply as Gassers. This class required full fenders, and gasoline for fuel. Throughout the late 1950s, the rules governing this class required that the supercharged cars be advanced one class. Supercharged cars were typically owned by the more serious racers. Even though they were advanced a class, they tended to be much faster than the unsupercharged, hopped-up street coupes they would usually run against. Also, the average hot street coupe didn't have its engine set back the allowable 10 percent that was permitted under the rules. In 1960 the NHRA made a revision to its rules, requiring Gas Coupes and Sedans to have full street equipment (lights, upholstery, and mufflers) and be self-starting (i.e., no push cars). Just as before, the classes were divided by cubic-inch-to-weight ratios, but now the supercharged cars were segregated into their own class. Now, unblown gas cars were designated simply by A/G, B/G, etc. Supercharged cars were now designated as A/GS for A Gas Supercharged, B/GS for B Gas Supercharged, and C/GS for C Gas Supercharged. This revised class structure separating the supercharged coupes into their own class gave racing fans some of the most intense competition ever seen on the strip.

The first real hero in the A/Gas Supercharged ranks was "Ohio" George Montgomery. In 1959 his Cadillac-powered 1933 Willys coupe recorded the fastest time of the year at 132.65 miles per hour. Only six years earlier, Montgomery made his first pass down a strip in his new 1953 Cadillac, turning a speed of 81.30 miles per hour. The Willys that Montgomery ran was found in a junkyard and purchased for $150. Selected for its short wheelbase and light weight, the Willys replaced the 1934 Ford coupe he had been running. Montgomery also upgraded the Caddy engine with a GMC-671 blower. Montgomery was a machinist by trade, and he made many of the components to adapt the blower to his Cadillac engine. In August 1959, Montgomery completed his baby blue Willys and made the short drive north to the NHRA Nationals in Detroit. His Cadillac engine was backed by a Cad/LaSalle transmission and a 1948 Ford rear end with a new set of M&H slicks. He handily won the A/Gas class and Little Eliminator honors.

In 1960, "Ohio" George returned to Detroit for another shot at the biggest race of the year. This time he baffled the

Tony Nancy's second roadster was more beautiful than the first. And, like the first, this one graced the cover of *Hot Rod* magazine. Nancy decided on a Buick V-8 for this roadster because he wanted something different. In addition, he wanted an engine that could be bored and stroked to increase its displacement.

In addition to building cars that looked good, Tony Nancy's cars always ran well too. By the time he was running at the 1961 Winternationals, he had added a 671 GMC blower with Enderly injectors. This combination on gas allowed him to run as fast as 144 miles per hour. *Tony Nancy collection*

Tony Nancy's modified roadster was built on a 102-inch dragster chassis with a fiberglass roadster body. Nancy is seen here fitting the aluminum seat while the car was under construction at his shop.
Tony Nancy collection

tech crews with the new coil-over front suspension on his Willys. Montgomery handily won the new A/Gas Supercharged class, setting both ends of the class record at 11.53 seconds and 130.57 miles per hour. In addition, he also claimed the Little Eliminator title. At this meet he had his car jacked up in the front and rear. This would be the trend for the Gassers through the early 1960s. This bias toward high center of gravity cars was something that the Ramchargers started a few years earlier with their *High & Mighty* coupe. The theory was that the higher the car's center of gravity, the more weight would be transferred to the rear wheels upon acceleration. The sky-high attitude of these cars looked aggressive and provided a good show for the fans as the cars bounced out of the chute. But their poor handling was a concern for the rule makers. In 1961 the NHRA limited the track-to-crankshaft height to 24 inches, which brought the cars down to a reasonable level and improved handling.

Because of Montgomery's dominance of A/Gas Supercharged, he became the poster boy for the Gasser class. This also brought more attention to the Willys body. Previously, Ford coupes had been the favorite of both drag racers and hot rodders. As the competition level rose, racers paid attention to every detail. Soon style gave way to speed and the Willys was seen as *the* Gasser. The frog became a prince, once builders realized that the Willys was lighter, had a short wheelbase, and could be had for a song as compared to the Ford bodies. Both the boxy 1933 Willys and the more streamlined 1940 Willys

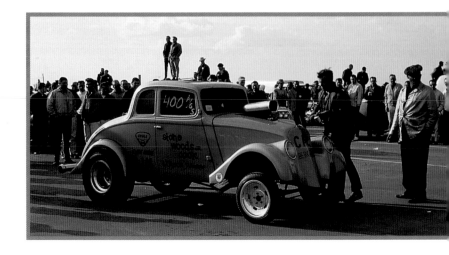

The Buick engine that Nancy had in his Model A roadster was installed in this modified roadster. Running in the A/Modified Roadster class, this car ran the quarter at speeds in excess of 170 miles per hour. As on his two other race cars, the number 22Jr. was painted on the side. *Tony Nancy collection*

Throughout the 1960s, A/Gas Supercharged was at the top of the gasser food chain. The team of Stone, Woods, and Cook successfully raced both the 1933 Willys seen here and a 1940 version. The rear bumper is a large steel pipe (probably filled with lead). *Pete Garramone*

were popular in the Gasser classes. Many of the Willys Gassers that ran as 1933 models were built with bodies from 1933 through 1936 cars. The 1940 Willys Gassers were actually 1937 to 1942 bodies with a fiberglass 1940 front end. Even though they were 100 pounds heavier and slightly larger than the 1933 through 1936 models, the 1940-style Willys typically ran quicker. In 1933 or 1940 form, the Willys became the icon for Gassers during the 1960s.

With the exception of George Montgomery's Cadillac-powered Willys, the most popular engine for the Supercharged A/Gassers was an Oldsmobile. It wasn't until John Mazmanian installed a Hemi in his 1940 Willys that anyone thought they would be practical for a Gasser. The cars in the lower Gas classes were usually powered by small-block Chevys. Regardless of engine choice, by the end of 1961, all of the big names in Gassers were running Hydra-matic transmissions. This was a big change, because a few years earlier, no racer worth his salt would have been caught dead racing a car with an automatic. B&M and Cal-Hydro were the two leading suppliers of four-speed Hydramatics for Gassers. Another automatic transmission that saw Gasser service was the Chrysler TorqueFlite, which had been successfully run in Dodge and Plymouth Super Stocks.

In the early- and mid-1960s, several top teams were successfully running Gassers. Names such as Stone-Woods & Cook,

Junior Thompson, Mallicoat Brothers, John Mazmanian, K.S. Pittman, and George Montgomery were drawing as big a following as many of the top dragster drivers. There were a lot of drag strips across the country and a lot of Gasser match races. This on-track competition boiled over to a war of words where challenges, claims, and counterclaims were spelled out in the drag-racing trade papers and enthusiast magazines. Ads for B&M Hydros, Isky cams, and Howard's Cams all made claims of speed and low elapsed times for the cars running their equipment. This media hype helped to sell tickets for match races.

The last major change to the Gassers came in 1965, when foreign-made bodies were included in the class. Initially, the NHRA rules excluded foreign-made cars, but other sanctioning bodies welcomed them. The most popular of these was the lightweight Anglia. George Montgomery ran one with Chevy power under Hurst sponsorship.

In 1966, Gassers had a new threat to their popularity—Funny Cars. The Funny Cars ran late model American-made bodies and burned nitro. They were much faster than the Gassers and drew a large following. It was also in the late 1960s that the "hot rod" image of the older coupes was fading in favor of Corvette, Opel GT, and Mustang Gassers. In the early 1970s, the dividing line between Funny Cars and Gassers was getting thin, and in 1975 the Gasser class was laid to rest.

John Mazmanian's beautiful candy apple 1940 Willys was the first to run a supercharged Chrysler Hemi. Up until Mazmanian's Hemi installation, nearly everyone thought the Hemi was for fuel-burning dragsters only. Several drivers handled this car, but Bob "Bones" Balogh is behind the wheel in this photo. *Pete Garramone*

In 1965, Gene Moody, owner and driver of this 1955 Chevy, was the D/Gas record holder. At that time, the 1955 Chevy was much like the 1932 Ford had been 10 years earlier. They were inexpensive to purchase and easy to modify into a winning gasser. *Larry Davis*

Jack "The Bear" Coonrod built and raced this 1933 Willys on tour against all the other big names in A/Gas Supercharged in 1967 and 1968. Here, the one-piece fiberglass front end has been removed, exposing the supercharged Chrysler Hemi engine. Coonrod's best speed in this car was 165.13 miles per hour. *Dave Crane collection*

ABOVE, RIGHT:
K. S. "Tiger" Pittman ran several different Willys gassers throughout the 1960s. The high stance of the Gassers, like this 1941 Willys, was established by George Montgomery's 1933 Willys. The car's height, extreme power, and short wheelbase made for visually exciting runs.

RIGHT:
One of the preferred engine combinations for the A/Gas supercharged cars of the early 1960s was the Oldsmobile backed by a B&M Hydro. The downward-facing headers that exited at the rear of the front tire were also typical on Willys gassers. When the cars accelerated, the headers added to the visual impact by blowing dust up from the surface of the track.

Races between fuel-burning altered coupes and roadsters were common spectacles in the late 1950s and early 1960s, primarily in Southern California. It was natural that the first generation of these coupes and roadsters would be fitted with fuel-burning dragster engines. Gene Mooneyham had been a regular, running as fast as 120 miles per hour. For running at the strip, he changed rear-end gears and added a little nitro. But an accident at San Diego's Paradise Mesa drag strip convinced Mooneyham that he should retire from driving. When he rebuilt his coupe he chopped the top, added a supercharger to the Chrysler

Hemi engine, and asked Larry Faust to drive. The blue coupe wore the numbers 554—numbers that would soon become famous.

Previously, Faust had driven flathead and Olds-powered roadsters on gas. "I think it ran 140," recalls Faust. "This coupe was a lot different!" Faust's first trial ride in the coupe ended after a few short passes, because of a broken rocker arm. The speed and roar of the fuel-burning Hemi, along with its unpredictable handling, made it a handful to drive. "The car never did the same thing twice," says Faust. "It would go left one time and right the next. It would hook up different, because it smoked the tires pretty hard." As with most early race cars, the 554 coupe had a few minor fires. Soon Faust was wearing a new fire suit. "When I got my first fire suit, it had a full mask with the breathers," says Faust. "When I went to make the first pass—the thing just didn't run." Mooneyham realized that with the full face mask Faust was not driving the same. The car sounded different to Faust when he wore the mask. "I was so used to hearing all the noise and what everything sounded like, that with the full face mask on, I couldn't hear anything. So, I cut the ear holes out and everything ran all right."

Mooneyham's coupe was consistently ranked first on the *Drag News* Junior Eliminator list. It was constantly booked for match races and challenges for the Number One spot on that list. The fans loved Mooneyham's coupe and would turn out to see the tire-smoking duels between it and its challenger. Eventually, he sold it and moved on to fuel dragsters.

Drag-racing legend John Force even had his chance to drive a fuel altered. He claims it was the first "real" race car he ever owned. Like most racers with cars that need a push start, Force used his Bell Gardens, California, neighborhood streets to shake down the car. "It never started," exclaimed Force. "We'd shove it and it just wouldn't start." One time while attempting a start, it did fire—and the throttle stuck. "That s.o.b. fired by pure accident and just took off," recalls Force. "Luckily, I put on the seat belt, but no fire suit or helmet." The car shot down the street with Force holding on for dear life. It passed his high school at high speed and then hit the railroad tracks which launched it into the air. It rolled end over end, over a fence, and into a yard in front of a house. Force climbed out unhurt. "The cops came and asked me what happened," says Force. "But by then, we had the trailer down there and were starting to load it up. I told them we were towing by here and the car came off the trailer and it went over the fence." Force obviously had a way with words back then, because the police believed him. "I was just a goofy old kid that just wanted to race."

After a successful year with an injected Chevy, the Kohler brothers installed a supercharged big-block Chevy in their Anglia and continued their winning ways. The success of this car convinced many Willys owners that the smaller Anglia was a better car for the Gasser classes. Although, because of the NHRA's 92-inch wheelbase minimum, the two-door Anglias could not legally compete in the supercharged gasser classes. *Dave Crane collection*

"Ohio" George Montgomery recognized the benefits of an Anglia body, and built this four-door version in 1965. It was powered by a supercharged small-block Chevy and sponsored by Hurst. It was legal for NHRA competition in A/Gas Supercharged class because of its 94-inch wheelbase. The car raced in both the gasser class and as an altered. Here at the 1966 U.S. Nationals, it is entered in BB/Altered. *Larry Davis*

Junior Thompson was another of the strong runners in A/Gas Supercharged. In 1965 he parked his Willys for this smaller 1950 Austin. In 1966 at Fremont, California, this car ran the quarter in 9.17 seconds at a speed of 155.85. *Bill Pitts*

The Lutz and Lunberg A/Gas Anglia is about to do a burn-out through rosin that has been spread on the track. This ritual was part of the prerace buildup prior to a match race against another gasser. In the background, parked at the base of the tower, is the track's own Cadillac ambulance. *Norm Kraus collection*

Another hot rod class was designated for "Altereds." The rules for these cars were a little less stringent than those for the Gas Coupes. The engines could be set back farther (25 percent) and very little was required in the way of running gear. In the late 1950s, one of the hottest A/Altereds was driven by Walt Knoch—*Walt's Puffer II*. It was a blown Hemi Chrysler-powered 1939 Fiat, built in 1959 by Walt's father, Walt Sr., and Tom Redmond. Walt Sr. owned Walt's Auto Parts in Inkster, Michigan. The car ran at the nearby Detroit Dragway and at a few other regional strips. The car ran well, but Knoch felt it needed to be upgraded for competition at the upcoming Nationals. "I told my dad," recalls Knoch, "there's no way we can run 140 with the Latham supercharger we had. I called Isky and Hilborn for the camshaft and injectors we needed. I got the injectors, supercharger, blower drive, and camshaft one week before 1959 Nationals." Knoch took the Fiat to a strip in Toledo and found that he could now smoke the tires for the entire length of the strip. "We went to the Nationals and on the first run, I broke the record." Knoch set the NHRA class speed record for A/Altered at 138.67 miles per hour. Following that meet, he went on to hit 150 miles per hour at a strip in Chester, South Carolina.

In 1960, Knoch returned to the Nationals, but lost the class to the Ratican-Jackson-Stearns Olds-powered Fiat. The latter repeated its class victory in the 1961 Nationals. Knoch's coupe, sporting a freshly chopped top, was running elapsed times in the 10-second range at speeds in excess of 150 miles per hour. The bright spot for the crew was the Middle Eliminator win for the other car they were running—a Chrysler-powered A/Roadster, named *Walt's Puffer Too*.

In 1962 the stars shined brightly for both cars at the U.S. Nationals. *Walt's Puffer Too* won the A/Roadster class and *Walt's Puffer II* won the A/Altered class. When the time came for the Junior Eliminator run between both cars, it was raining. With only the two *Walt's Puffer* cars to run against each other, it was assured that one of Knoch's cars would win. The trophy was awarded to Knoch and the record books read "Walt's Puffers."

NHRA SAFETY SAFARI

In 1954 the NHRA sent a group of traveling drag-racing evangelists on the road and named them the Safety Safari. Under the guidance of E. J. "Bud" Coons, the Safety Safari was charged with assisting groups across the nation in establishing local drag-racing events, to "show-how with know-how." Coons' initial contact with hot rodding came in 1949, when, as a traffic officer for the city of Pomona, California, he was appointed the department's liaison to the local hot rod clubs. Coons found himself more intrigued by the racing world than with his duties as a police officer. In the spring of 1954, Coons and his three-man crew of race organizational experts hit the road in their Plymouth station wagon, pulling a small travel trailer. They carried everything they needed to set up a first class drag-racing event. This small band of drag-racing specialists knew there were a lot of fast cars across the nation and their goal was to provide a safe environment for them to race.

Abandoned airstrips were a favorite location for drag-racing events. They were long, straight, and plentiful following World War II. A local hot rod club would work with the Safety Safari to organize the affair. The Safari brought timing devices, car classification and inspection gear, and course measuring equipment. In addition, it brought a wealth of knowledge that it passed on to the local organizers. As a former law enforcement officer, Coons carried instant credibility to the local police agencies where these events were staged. During the 1954 tour, the Safety Safari conducted 10 meets in as many states.

In 1955 the Safari received a sponsorship from the Mobil Oil Company. The NHRA's roving ambassadors had higher aspirations for the tour's sophomore year, and they met their goals. Much of the public relations work done in 1954 paid big dividends in 1955, with 19 events staged. In Kansas City, Missouri, the Safari conducted a regional event at the first strip built expressly for drag racing. Other firsts during the Safari's 1955 tour were inaugural events in Indianapolis, Indiana; Columbus, Ohio; and Allentown, Pennsylvania.

In 1956 the Safari, now a five-man team, hit the road again in a new Plymouth Fury wagon, pulling the now-familiar red-and-white NHRA trailer. In addition to establishing new facilities, it was their goal to conduct two-day regional events across the country. The culmination of the 1956 tour was the Second Annual National Championship Drag Races, held in Kansas City, Missouri. The 352 entrants came from almost all of the then-48 states, Canada, and Hawaii. This was a four-day event.

The 1956 tour was the Safari's last. The legacy left by Bud Coons and the other Safari members is enormous. Without their missionary work in providing a safe, controlled environment for drag racers, the sport might not have seen the rapid nationwide growth and public acceptance that it did in those formative years.

In 1954, Bud Coons headed a small group of specialists that crossed the country in this Plymouth station wagon pulling a small travel trailer. These drag-racing evangelists carried everything with them to put on an organized drag race except the pavement. It was because of their efforts that thousands of people were exposed to drag racing in the 1950s. *Don Cox*

Mooneyham's 1934 Ford coupe was powered by a supercharged Chrysler Hemi engine. It was set back in the chassis 25 percent and drove directly to the rear end without a transmission.

Rich Guasco's *Pure Hell* set the world of Fuel Altereds on its collective ear in 1964, when it ran a string of eight consecutive runs under nine seconds. These runs proved that a lightweight car with a Chevy engine could compete against the Chrysler Hemis. This photo was taken at the 1965 March Meet. Dale Emery, in a full firesuit, is behind the wheel. *Bill Pitts*

By now, the Walt's Puffer Fiat was assuming legendary status in the Midwest. So much so that when AMT released its Fiat model car kit, it carried the 285 number on the side—the same as *Walt's Puffer II*. In 1963 the NHRA realigned its divisions. This realignment, and the younger Knoch's temper, would cause him some problems at the 1963 Nationals.

When Knoch ran time trials in the *Walt's Puffer II* A/Altered Fiat at the 1963 Nationals, his time slips were blank—no time or speed. Jack Chrisman was standing on the starting line and said to Knoch, "Damn, you got your car running really good." Chrisman told Knoch he was running in the 9.60 range. Knoch wanted to know how Chrisman knew the times when his slips were blank. Chrisman explained he was in the tower and saw the times. He encouraged Knoch to go to the tower and find out what the problem was. "I walked in, and Eileen Daniels [wife of Bob Daniels, NHRA's Division 3 director] was there," says Knoch. "I told her I wanted to see the times that I ran. She started to give them to me and then this woman in a red jump suit came over and said, 'Are you Walt Knoch with the Walt's Puffer cars?'" After Knoch confirmed his identity, the woman in red instructed Daniels not to give Knoch any of his times. A divisional realignment changed the numbering system for the A/Altered cars, and the NHRA had assigned Knoch's Fiat the number 385. Knoch wanted to retain the 285 number that had been on his car for years and was also on the AMT model.

Knoch was directed upstairs, where he could plead his case to Wally Parks (NHRA President) and Ed Eaton (NHRA's competition director). "Eaton and Wally Parks both disagreed with my point of view—I was right and they were wrong," says Knoch. Unfortunately for Knoch, Parks and Eaton had control of the event. The next time Knoch pulled up to the line to race, he was given the cut signal and not allowed to run. An irate Knoch stormed to the tower. "The timing tower was probably three or four stories high and they had a couple of security cops at the bottom of the stairs," says Knoch. The two guards asked Knoch where he was going, and told him he couldn't go up the stairs. "One guy stood up and took a swing at me, or something like that, and bam-bam—two guys were down on the ground—I went upstairs." Someone yelled, "Get this guy out of here!" and two Indiana state troopers grabbed Knoch. Before he could be escorted out, Knoch was asked to go upstairs. "I went upstairs with the cops following me. Wally Parks and Ed Eaton were up there—they read me the riot act." Knoch was thrown out of the event and the troopers were asked to escort him out. Walt Knoch's driving career ended in 1963 when NHRA approached his father and told him, "We'll allow your cars to run, but your kid can't drive 'em." Knoch then got involved in drag boats.

Another Detroit area competitor in the Altered class was Elwood Peterson. In 1959 he and friends Gordon McNuff and Bruce Boyce decided to build a car for the upcoming U.S.

Ed Hollis ran this Fiat in C/Altered in the early 1960s. It looks as though it was built on a set of early frame rails. The engine is a small-block Chevy with six two-barrel carburetors. An interesting detail on this car is the way the body is hinged at the rear. Hollis appears to be ahead of his time with this type of body mount. *James Genat/Zone Five Photo*

Running nitromethane in coupes became a passion in Southern California in the late 1950s. The most famous of the Fuel Coupes was Gene Mooneyham's 554 coupe. Driven by Larry Faust, it consistently headed *Drag News'* Eliminator list. In 1960 it was the first Fuel Coupe to run 150 miles per hour.

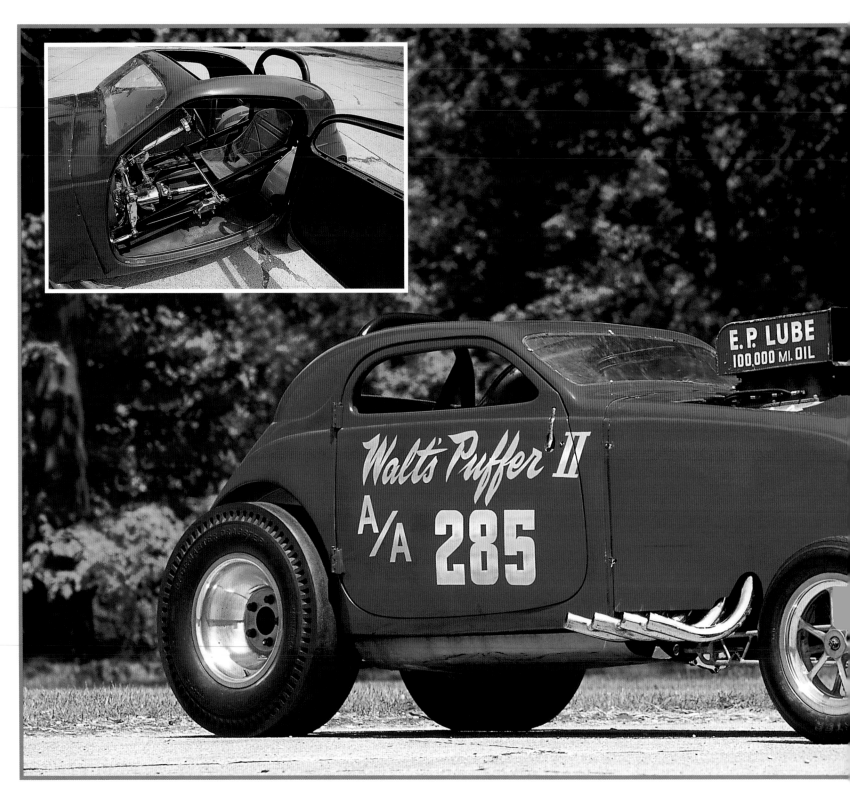

ABOVE:

In the mid-1950s, some guys would race anything. The Oilers club of Carlsbad, California, brought this heavily chopped Crosley to a meet in Colton, California. At that time, narrowing the rear axle was not perceived as a benefit to the handling of a drag-race car. *Don Cox*

LEFT:

Shortly before the 1959 U.S. Nationals, *Walt's Puffer II* received a major mechanical overhaul that included a new camshaft, supercharger, and injectors for its Chrysler Hemi engine. On the first run it broke the NHRA's A/Altered speed record, at 138.67 miles per hour.

INSET:

The frame for the *Walt's Puffer II* A/Altered Fiat was made from rectangular steel tubing. The seat is a surplus aircraft unit and the steering column and wheel are from a Corvette. The chrome handle to the left of the driver's seat is for the brakes.

Elwood Peterson helped build and race this chopped Crosley altered, which ran its first national event at the 1959 U.S. Nationals. Since that time, the car has been updated to comply with current safety rules, and it still competes today. Years ago, it was named the *Blue Goose*, because of its ungainly looks.

Between 1960 and 1970, Altered coupes went from junkyard frame rails, to homemade frames built from steel tubing, to professionally built race car chassis. In 1970, Logghe Stamping built this chassis for the Altered class. It featured all the suspension technology of the Funny Car chassis it was selling at the time. The Fiat body fitted to this frame is made of fiberglass, lighter, stronger, and less expensive than its steel counterpart. *John Logghe collection*

Nationals. They settled on a 1947 Crosley body that had been parked alongside the fence at a local junkyard. Peterson had previously used the body as a stepladder to get over that fence and into the yard. For a total cost of $15 he had the start to his Altered. They built a frame out of 2-1/4-inch tubing with a Crosley front axle and a 1939 Ford rear axle. The body was chopped 6 inches, the cowl was shortened, and a Model A deck lid was used for the rear roll pan. The 1957 Olds engine came from partner Boyce. They fitted the car with deep blue tinted glass. Upon completion, someone looked at the car and said it was as ugly as a blue goose! The name stuck. While its performance at the 1959 Nationals was not spectacular, it did manage to be runner-up in B/Altered at both the 1962 and 1963 Nationals.

Eventually the *Goose's* Olds was swapped for a small-block Chevy and even ran with a small amount of nitro, running its best time of 9.47 seconds at 148 miles per hour. In 1994 the *Goose* ran at the 40th U.S. Nationals at Indy. When most race cars have long since been placed in a retirement home, the *Goose* has been updated to current safety standards and is still going strong, running nostalgia races on the Goodguy circuit.

BIBLIOGRAPHY

Magazine & Periodical Articles

" '60 National Drag Championships." *Hot Rod* (December 1960).

"1962 Winternational Championship Drags." *Hot Rod* (May 1962).

"22 JR." *Rodders Journal* (Winter 1995).

"30 Years of NHRA Pro Stock." *Car Craft* (June 2000).

"40 Years of Drag Racing Coverage - 1970." *National Dragster* (May 28, 1999).

"40 Years of Drag Racing Coverage - 1971." *National Dragster* (June 4, 1999).

"8.09 Special." *Hot Rod* (December 1962).

"A Sense of Tradition." *Popular Hot Rodding* (February 2000).

"Best Engineered, '63 Winternationals." *Hot Rod* (September 1963).

"Dean Moon's Mooneyes." *Popular Hot Rodding* (November 1962).

"Drag Racing, Evolution of the Sport." *Car Life* (September 1962).

"Dragmaster Dart." *Car Life* (September 1962).

"Dual Challenger." *Custom Rodder* (January 1958).

"Ford's 90-Day Wonder." *Hot Rod* (January 1965).

"Fuel City U.S.A." *Hot Rod* (May 1965).

"GM Rivalry." *Automobile Quarterly* (Winter 1992).

"Grumpy's Toy." *Hot Rod* (December 1975).

"Hot Rodding's Biggest Merger." *Rod Builder & Customizer* (August 1958).

"Howard Cams Rattler." *Hot Rod* (August 1969).

"HRM Salutes the Vapor Trailers of Visalia, California." *Hot Rod* (May 1961).

"Ivo's Red Bomb." *Car Craft* (September 1960).

"King of the Drags." *Car Craft* (October 1959).

"Less Weight Means More Ford." *Hot Rod* (July 1963).

"Motor City Missile." *Hot Rod* (September 1961).

"Motor City Spectacular." *Hot Rod* (November 1959).

"Nationals Flash." *Hot Rod* (November 1960).

"NHRA Divisional Drags: Memphis, Tennessee." *Hot Rod* (August 1992).

"Old Race Cars Never Die." *The Corvette Restorer Magazine* (Winter 1999).

"Slick Slicks." *Rodding and Re-styling* (December 1957).

"Texas Tornado." *Hot Rod* (August 1962).

"The Big Go West." *Hot Rod* (May 1961).

"The Early Nationals Stockers." *National Dragster* (August 2000).

"The Gasser Warrior." *Hot Rod* (September 2000).

"The Tony Nancy Touch." *Hot Rod* (April 1960)

"Tony Tailors a Tiger." *Hot Rod* (August 1962).

"Top Eliminator: Jack Chrisman." *Hot Rod* (December 1962).

"Two-Thing"—Chevy with a Kicker." *Hot Rod* (February 1961).

"What Makes Grumpy Happy." *Hot Rod* (December 1972).

"Where Are They Now? Jim Nelson and Dode Martin." *National Dragster* (May 2000).

"Winternationals Drags." *Rod & Custom* (June 1962).

"Winternationals Number Ten." *Hot Rod* (April 1970).

"World Series of Drag Racing." *Rod & Custom* (January 1955).

Books

Batchelor, Dean. *The American Hot Rod*. Osceola, WI: MBI Publishing Company, 1995.

Editors of *Hot Rod* Magazine. *Drag Racing Pictorial*. Los Angeles, CA: Petersen Publishing Co., 1957.

Editors of *Hot Rod* Magazine. *Hot Rod Your Car*. Los Angeles, CA: Petersen Publishing Co., 1952.

Editors of *Hot Rod* Magazine. *Stock Cars for the Drags*. Los Angeles, CA: Petersen Publishing Co., 1963.

Garlits, Don. *'Big Daddy.'* Ocala, FL: Don Garlits Museum of Drag Racing, 1990.

Garlits, Don. *Big Daddy a Career Pictorial*. Ocala, FL: The Museum of Drag Racing, 1994.

Hill, George. *1956 Hot-Rod Handbook*. Chicago, IL: Popular Mechanics Company, 1956.

Lawlor, John. *Hot Rodding the Buick*. Los Angeles, CA: Petersen Publishing Co., 1964.

Martin, Chris. *The Top Fuel Handbook*. Wichita, KS: The Wichita Eagle and Beacon Publishing Co., 1996.

Montgomery, Don. *Supercharged Gas Coupes*. Fallbrook, CA: Don Montgomery, 1993.

Montgomery, Don. *Those Wild Fuel Altereds*. Fallbrook, CA: Don Montgomery, 1997.

Post, Robert. *High Performance*. Baltimore, MD: The Johns Hopkins University Press, 1994.